GROWING UP DIVORCED

GROWING UP DIVORCED

A ROAD TO HEALING FOR ADULT CHILDREN OF DIVORCE

Diane Fassel

POCKET BOOKS

New York   London   Toronto   Sydney   Tokyo   Singapore

POCKET BOOKS, a division of Simon & Schuster
1230 Avenue of the Americas, New York, NY 10020

Fassel, Diane.
   Growing up divorced : a road to healing for adult children of
divorce / Diane Fassel.
      p.   cm.
   Includes bibliographical references.
   ISBN 0-671-70009-X : $19.95
   1. Adult children of divorced parents—Mental health.   2. Adult
children of divorced parents—Rehabilitation.   I. Title.
RC569.5.A3F37   1991
155.9'24—dc20   90-47666
                                                          CIP

First Pocket Books hardcover printing February 1991

10 9 8 7 6 5 4 3 2 1

Printed in the U.S.A.

CONTENTS

For the adult children of divorce in this study who generously gave of themselves and their stories, and especially for my "kids," Roddy, Beth, Kate, and John.

ACKNOWLEDGMENTS

I am grateful for the assistance I received from many friends and associates. My agent, Jonathon Lazear, encouraged me to develop the idea of adult children of divorce when it was in seed form. When I bemoaned that it was "too hard and not enough is known about it," he just laughed and said, "I know you can do it." He was right and his belief in me facilitated my work. Linda Lewis organized the interview data, wading through massive amounts of material and turning it into a form I could use. Ann Sprague typed the bulk of the manuscript and added immeasurably to the book by her editing, which was always thoughtful, astute, and accurate. Mary Ann Wells pitched in at every deadline and typed some of the manuscript. Anne Wilson Schaef was the one who saw the need to broaden the concept of adult children of divorce so that it included the effect of society on how ACODs view themselves. She contributed greatly to my thinking about the myth of the intact family. Claire Zion, my editor, made me work harder on this book than on any previous book I've written. I have Claire to thank for helping me become a better writer and for taking such an active and personal interest in this book.

Since this is a book about family and the longing for family, I have been aware, during the writing, of my own family of origin. We were by no means perfect and we floundered under many of the strains discussed here. Yet slowly we are beginning our recovery, proving that it is never too late. I am so grateful to my family of origin for their willingness to face our family issues, and I feel proud to be part of the process with them. Finally, to my own family and extended family in Boulder, especially Anne and John, who are my loved ones in this adventure we call "living in process," thank you for your constant and loving support.

I

THE
LEGACY
OF
DIVORCE

1 Adult Children of Divorce—The Problems, the Challenge

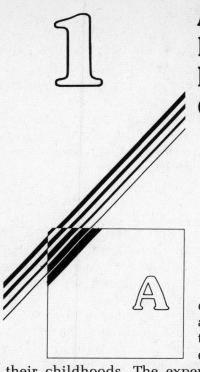

dult children of divorce (ACODs) are a vast portion of our population. They are persons whose parents divorced at some point in their childhoods. The experience of the divorce, while intended to improve life for at least one parent and the children, frequently had the opposite effect. Children felt abandoned, isolated, responsible, and fearful. These and other feelings were carried from childhood into adulthood. ACODs tend to be trapped in outmoded survival behaviors that helped them as children but that prove disastrous in their adult relationships.

There is growing interest in the effects of divorce on children, and new studies are beginning to document these effects. Unfortunately, little is known about ACODs. I decided to write this book because of my conviction that ACOD issues need to be named and identified. My interest in ACOD issues is both personal and professional. Although I am not an ACOD, I worked for many years as a divorce and child-custody mediator.

Mediators are neutral third parties who facilitate a divorce, helping the divorcing couple to develop an agreement

3

for the division of property and—if they are parents—for a child-custody arrangement. Divorcing couples frequently seek the aid of a mediator to avoid the interference of lawyers, who often prove adversarial and expensive. Mediation is based on the belief that in the majority of cases, the disputing parties are the ones who should determine what custody arrangement is in the best interest of their children. Over the years, I have assisted many families throughout the breakup of marriage and the difficult decisions involving child custody. I was highly committed to my work; nevertheless, I wondered about the effects of divorce on the children in later life.

I still remember an especially poignant evening when I met with a family to finalize their custody agreement. Earlier, I had met with the parents to work out all the legal details, and this evening we were sharing the information with the four children. In every respect, the gathering seemed ideal. The parents, Cliff and Marge, spoke of their love for their children. They acknowledged their pain at separating and at changing their children's lives. They assured their children that they would be cared for and that their lives would continue with a minimum of disruption. The children, three boys and a girl, sat mute and tearful. I asked them if they had questions, did they wish to say anything? They shook their heads no. We completed the documents and I rose to leave. Suddenly, the youngest, four-year-old Cassie, flung herself around my legs, shaking with big, deep sobs. I gathered her into my arms as she cried, "Don't let my mommy and daddy do this!"

Abruptly, our little signing felt painful and bleak. I left the newly divorced family, all now as tearful as Cassie. I drove home with a lump in my throat and a tight fist around my stomach. After years of facilitating families through their divorce agreements, I had to acknowledge that even the "best" divorces are painful and traumatic, especially for the children. I have frequently wondered what happened to Cassie. She is someone whose pain has stayed with me over the years.

It is a fact that divorce has become the norm for our society. Beginning in 1970, the divorce rate peaked, occurring in one out of every two marriages. This statistic has remained constant into the 1990s. Thirty-eight percent of all children will experience the divorce of their parents or as the result of divorce, will live in a single-parent household before the age of eighteen. The statistics regarding multiple divorce rise for children born in the 1980s. One-half of these children will experience their parents' divorce. In the cases where mothers remarry, half of these remarriages end in a second divorce. Thus, these children will have experienced a second family disruption before the age of sixteen.[1]

Research on divorce indicates that divorce is almost always a traumatic experience for children. Children feel fear, grief, guilt, loss, and abandonment. The few longitudinal studies that exist claim that the effects of divorce appear to be long lasting, not temporary as had previously been thought. It is fortunate that more attention is now being given to studying the effects of divorce on children. However, when we turn our attention to adults who experienced, as children, their parents' divorce, we are met with silence. There is almost nothing written on this topic. With few exceptions, most research is about the effects of divorce on children, not on adults who came from divorced families. The closest any researchers come are Judith Wallerstein and Sandra Blakeslee in their book *Second Chances*, which is a study of sixty divorced families over a period of ten years.[2]

I decided to walk into this informational void and to learn everything I could about adult children of divorce. My research was qualitative. I did not begin with a hypothesis but with a question: What was the ACOD experience? As there was little research in existence, I began with a series of interviews of persons between the ages of twenty and sixty-two whose parents had divorced. The interviews were exploratory and open-ended. I wanted to know if ACODs had anything in common. The interviewees, in turn, described their childhood experiences and the major issues they were facing as adults. They spoke with a frankness I had not anticipated. Many of them had spent long hours pondering the source of their feelings. Frequently, they turned to the experience of their parents' divorce as the beginning of their difficulties.

From these interviews, which were mainly anecdotal, I began to discern a set of characteristics that occurred in almost everyone's story. I listed these characteristics and several other questions and formulated a survey, which I sent to 350 randomly selected people in the United States and Canada. A few questionnaires were sent to Germany and Austria as well. I asked those who filled out the survey to respond from their own experience.

Nothing prepared me for the kind of response I received to the survey. Questionnaires were promptly returned. They were thoroughly filled out. In fact, extra sheets of paper were added to some, with expanded detail. Many respondents said the questionnaire itself helped them name issues they had struggled with all their lives. My office received requests for more questionnaires so that respondents could share them with family and friends. Almost everyone agreed to a follow-up interview. Persons I had never met phoned me and insisted they be interviewed for the book. One man called and demanded that I hear his story. Everywhere I went (and I travel widely for my work, which includes organizational consulting in addition to mediation), people willingly agreed to an interview. They shared their stories eagerly, and with an intensity I rarely experience in doing research. Obviously, I had tapped into a caldron of high feelings on the part of these adult children of divorce.

Writing a book on ACODs changed my thinking in dramatic ways. I was confronted with the fact that not all divorces are alike. In fact, to think of divorce as an isolated event is a misconception. If I have learned anything from my research, it is that divorce is a process. Divorce begins well before the actual split and leads to the need for a separation. Then there is the separation itself, followed by the aftermath, which can go on for years. ACODs are affected by the entire process of the divorce, not just the fact of a separation. There are numerous ways in which the process of divorce is carried out. The process itself is crucial to how ACODs perceive themselves and the issues they must confront in adulthood.

A forty-year-old female ACOD (her parents divorced when she was six), who is herself divorced with two teenagers, confided that she had feared abandonment all her life. She formed liaisons with people who left her, thus fulfilling her deepest fear. Her first abandonment occurred when her parents divorced and her mother disappeared overnight, never to return, even for a visit.

Obviously, children who had a "disappearing" parent

have different issues from children who witnessed constant fighting. In the course of my research I identified five types of divorce and their characteristics. While some people may have unique experiences that do not fall neatly into one of my categories, I find them useful because these five occurred regularly in my interviews: the disappearing parent, the surprise divorce, the always-fighting divorce, the let's-keep-this-from-the-kids divorce, and the late-in-life divorce.

Not only does each type of divorce engender different issues for the ACOD, but the ACOD's age at the time of the parents' divorce also seems to affect the issues to be faced later in life.

Adult children of divorce do have many common characteristics. First and foremost, they share an experience: At some point in their lives, their parents divorced. This event affected all of them in long-lasting ways. Regardless of whether they were one year old or twenty-two years old when it occurred, the divorce heralded irrevocable changes.

Throughout life, ACODs find themselves reacting in fairly predictable ways. They have an overdeveloped sense of responsibility. They fear conflict, yet use it in their relationships. They are easily drawn into taking sides, all the while feeling uncomfortable. They feel abandoned, whether or not they are in reality. They abandon others themselves. They feel used in personal relationships and in work settings. Often, they create the conditions by which they let themselves be used. ACODs feel helpless. Lacking some communication and social skills, they stand by watching in situations that call for action. They seek a home. Although many ACODs have achieved economic security, there is still the ever-present fear that they could lose their security overnight. Authority figures are sources of anxiety for ACODs. Either idealized or blamed, authorities are invested with expectations that ACODs had for their parents. Struggling with control, ACODs find that relationships fail because of their excessive controlling behaviors. They have unrealistic expectations for their relationships. Marriages are entered into with rigid requirements. Intimacy, always elusive, is sometimes not risked at all by ACODs. These characteristics and others are discussed in Part I, where I attempt to identify and define the ACOD phenomenon.

In the second section of this book, I consider the good

news about ACODs. Not all divorces were negative. Some were positive solutions to dysfunctional situations. Some ACODs learned valuable skills. Others saw they had options for their lives; they do not have to stay in unhealthy situations. Many ACODs developed independence, flexibility, and self-reliance, characteristics they would never have developed if they had not been tested by the divorce.

Recovery is possible for ACODs. Like divorce, healing from the effects of divorce is also a process. Fortunately, we live in a time when many types of self-help books and groups are available. Because I know of no specific groups devoted solely to ACOD recovery, later in the book I propose how such groups could be formed, using reliable methods from the self-help movement.

Finally, in the last chapters of the book, I turn away from the microscopic examination of ACOD issues to larger, societal issues. If ACODs teach us anything, it is that divorce is a process within the larger process of the dysfunctional family, within the still larger process of dysfunctional society. Surprisingly, as I wrote this book, I was often approached by persons who insisted they had the same characteristics as ACODs, even though they lived in nondivorcing families. Upon examination, it became clear that many of these people had parents who were legally married, but felt emotionally separated because of years of family dysfunction. While these people were not ACODs and experienced many different issues, they did help me identify the important role society plays in our perception and experience of divorce.

I believe society perpetuates the myth of the intact family as a way of remaining in denial about the fact that divorce has now become common. We are taught to think dualistically: marriage and long-term commitments are good, divorce is bad. Yet, evidence from my interviews and the opinion of many other commentators suggest that the traditional family unit— mom, pop, two kids—is in trouble. However, the degree of guilt, shame, and blame that ACODs carry convinces me that we persist in believing we *should* be able to create intact families that stick it out through thick and thin. I believe that many ACODs are casualties of this kind of attitude in society. Consequently, it is important to recognize that ACOD recovery is not just for the individual. Individual ACODs must heal, but at some level society itself must heal. Our cultural myths must change, lest we perpetuate expectations under which a large portion of our population collapses.

In the course of writing this book, I often found myself questioning the characteristics I had assigned solely to ACODs. Are not ACODs just products of dysfunctional families? In some cases, aren't they adult children of addictive families (ACOAs)? Both are true. ACODs do tend to carry many of the characteristics of adult children of dysfunctional families. In addition, alcoholism, drugs, workaholism, relationship and sex addictions (to name a few) were often present in ACOD families.

Nevertheless, for people who identify themselves as ACODs, divorce is the central event within the larger process of the dysfunctional family. It is the hub around which everything else turns. It is the process of divorce to which ACODs return when they want to see what they learned about guilt, abandonment, and fear. The divorce was the context for ACODs taking various roles in the family, with some becoming heroes, others scapegoats, or lost children or mascots. It is the divorce they remember when they discuss their troubles with intimate relationships or when they back off from making a commitment.

In no way is the ACOD perspective a "single issue" phenomenon. Undoubtedly, many ACODs can benefit by learning more about their addictive and dysfunctional family patterns. But to the extent that divorce was the key process in their lives, that issue causes them the worst trouble and needs to be "worked" first.

I began researching the topic of ACODs for reasons that I thought were professional, but that quickly became personal. As a divorce and child-custody mediator, I thought it would help me understand what happened to the children in all the families whose divorces I mediated. I learned something about that, and I contacted, at a personal level, the pain, frustration, and struggle of so many who shared their stories with me. I believe their willingness to share their experience through the medium of this book is itself redemptive of the experience of being an ACOD. Through it all, I have become more firmly convinced that ACODs have real problems and real issues related to the impact of the divorce process that deserve to be named and addressed. I hope that ACODs gain relief in finding their experience identified here. I hope they no longer feel alone as so many say they have for so many years. I trust ACODs will use this book to aid their healing, remembering that their past does not necessarily predetermine their present or their future.

Finally, I believe that the plight of ACODs is symptomatic of a deeper problem, a more pervasive denial in our society. I wrote this book to examine both issues—the individual and the societal—and to suggest processes that lead to greater health for both.

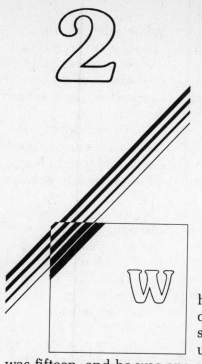

Divorce and Dysfunction— Untangling the Web

hen Phil telephoned with a sense of urgency in his voice, I responded more quickly than usual. I had known Phil since he was fifteen, and he was one of many teenagers who piled into my car for the obligatory chauffeuring that goes on before kids have their driver's licenses. Now Phil asked if he could meet me somewhere for a talk. He said he felt upset and troubled. We agreed to see each other over a cup of tea at a small cafe the next afternoon.

When I arrived at the cafe, I was surprised at the changes in Phil. He was no longer the boy I had remembered. At twenty-five, his body had filled out and he was not a lanky high school kid. We hugged each other and ordered our tea. After some small talk, Phil moved right into the reason for his call. "There's something I need to ask you," he began, his voice shaky. "Is there something wrong with me because my parents are divorced?" I was shocked by his question, and curious as to how the young man I had known as bright, lively, and loving had become so serious and sad in just ten years. I encouraged Phil to tell me more about himself and about how he had

11

judged himself dysfunctional as the result of his parents' divorce.

"Well," Phil began, "I think you know that my folks divorced during my first year of college. I had just turned eighteen. I wasn't all that surprised because there had been a lot of tension in our family for years, and it was kind of a relief to finally have it over. Dad wanted out of the marriage long before Mom did. They lived very separate lives until I graduated from high school. I think perhaps they stayed together for my sake. But now my problem is that I don't trust relationships. I meet girls I really like and just when we're beginning to get close, I break off the relationship. I feel terrified of closeness, but I'm lonely without relationships."

Phil continued, describing two relationships he had formed with young women. One relationship became very serious and they were considering marriage. "When it got to that point, I just freaked," Phil went on. "I got so crazy and rigid that I believed I had no options. I felt I either had to marry this woman or leave the relationship completely. I eventually made her so miserable, she broke it off. So she left me. Even though she asked me to stay with her without deciding one way or the other, I couldn't stand the uncertainty. I'm sick about what happened. I might not have wanted to marry her, but in the end I also lost a good friend, maybe my best friend." Phil paused. He stared into his teacup, swirled the liquid around. Then he gazed out the cafe window. Outside, it was white with a new-fallen snow. I waited. It didn't seem that Phil was finished. Finally, he looked back at me and said, "I didn't feel these kinds of problems with girlfriends before my folks divorced. Do you think their divorce caused this?"

I felt completely overwhelmed by Phil's question. Although I had spent the last year immersed in just such stories as Phil's, turning a microscopic gaze on the issues of ACODs, I now felt confounded by the "this" of Phil's question. Did divorce cause "this"? Did it turn a heretofore reasonably healthy teenager into a rigid, controlling, fearful young man who sabotaged his closest relationships?

Phil and I talked longer. I shared with him what I had been learning about ACODs. He seemed relieved to have a name for some of the things he was feeling. We parted several hours after we had met. The sun was going down over the mountains and the waiters had changed shifts at the cafe. I trudged to my car, more pensive than I had been before meeting with Phil. Obviously, in many people's minds (Phil's included), divorce was bad. Simplistically, yet understandably, he had concluded that without his parents' divorce, his life would be trouble free. Unfortunately, there is a shred of truth in Phil's thinking. But only a shred. Divorce had certainly been a focal point that brought to light years of distress in Phil's family. Yet divorce was the culmination of long-standing dysfunction. Even without divorce, Phil would have had many of the feelings he described. Divorce was the process that broke down the denial about the extent of dysfunction in Phil's family.

Before going any further, I believe it is necessary to understand the relationship between dysfunction and divorce. Dysfunction and divorce are not the same *and* sometimes they are related. Divorce is related to dysfunction in that the more controlling, angry, inexpressive, depressed, etc., a person is, the more impossible it is for such a person to relate with a spouse and children. In turn, the family system takes on its own dysfunction and begins to break down. In these cases, dysfunction causes divorce because the intimate relationship of marriage becomes intolerable.

Conversely, not all divorce is the result of dysfunction. Sometimes people grow apart. They actually become healthier and see that their marriage can no longer support their growth. In these cases, people separate amicably. I hope that clarifying the differences between divorce and dysfunction will make it easier to turn our attention to the unique issues of ACODs. Let's begin by looking at dysfunction.

Understanding Dysfunction

In order to gain a working definition of dysfunction, think of the term "dysfunction" as a large umbrella. Under the umbrella are various issues that are found in families today and that make family life unmanageable. These issues include any behaviors that are used as a substitute for intimacy and can include addictions, abuse, and emotional repression. Some examples of such behaviors are: the abuse of any addictive substances such as alcohol, drugs, and food; the abuse of addictive processes such as work, relationships, sex, spending, consuming, and religion, among others; and physical, sexual, and psychological and verbal abuse.

All three of these issues—addiction, abuse, and emotional repression—are, by definition, inherently dysfunctional. Addiction, abuse, and emotional repression differ from divorce, which can be beneficial or harmful depending upon how it is done, in that they create the conditions by which the family becomes progressively sicker. Violence, for example, does not have any justification in the family. Violence is profoundly disrespectful of another and violates personal boundaries. There is nothing positive about it. The family becomes dysfunctional because a requirement for belonging to the family is that members take on certain roles and these roles are neither freely chosen nor negotiable.

The family members cannot be themselves, and eventually, intimacy becomes impossible. At the root of all dysfunction is the inability to feel, the freezing of feelings, or the ignoring of feelings. Dysfunctional families are first and foremost places where it is not safe to feel.

Dysfunction in the individual and in the home is characterized by the following:

- denial about the family's reality.
- keeping secrets from oneself and others as to what is really going on in the family.
- taking on roles that are not appropriate for one's age or experience; for example, a nine-year-old girl who parents her younger siblings.
- an environment in which only certain expressions of feelings are allowed, others are prohibited; for example, the family in which the mother glared at her children as they left for their father's funeral, saying, "We don't cry in public, so pull yourselves together."
- communication that is vague, indirect, and triangulated, and in which members usually have to guess at what is meant; messages are carried by third parties and there is no sense that one is heard when

one speaks; most conversation becomes formalized, ritualized, or rote.
- lack of respect for personal limits, boundaries, and privacy; especially common in families where there is sexual abuse.
- anxiety prevails, playfulness is rare.
- control, extending to all areas of family life, in which rules govern such things as use of money, styles of clothes, housework, political orientations, etc. The purpose of the rules is to maintain a closed system.
- lack of self-identity, the sense that it is not okay to be different from the family; conversely, the family system is so closed that the outside world feels different and dangerous.

Because the family is a system, it is affected by each member. Thus, even when only one member is dysfunctional, the rest of the family begins to take on dysfunctional behaviors. Even benign issues can become dysfunctional. In a family where a teenage son was physically disabled as the result of an auto accident, the other family members put aside their own needs to care for him. Over the years, he became more dependent and they became more resentful, but no one dared speak their feelings because of "poor Joe." Joe grew addicted to pain medication. The family created a wall of denial. They refused to see Joe's growing addiction. Their excuse was that he had to be allowed some addictions after all he had suffered. Their caretaking became more rigid and regimented. The family would not recognize their need for rest and for space from Joe, so the only way they got relief was to become physically ill, which they did regularly.

This is a situation where the family simply stopped focusing on the needs of each member and made Joe their entire focus. When one member of the family becomes the family's sole focus, even when that person's needs are legitimate as Joe's needs were, the other members neglect themselves. Instead of confronting their feelings of being left out and their beliefs that they were unworthy of love and attention, they channeled their feelings into caretaking Joe. The imbalance in their system manifested itself in everybody's becoming sick. Rather than dealing with their guilt that they could walk and Joe could not, they made themselves miserable. They became as emotionally dysfunctional as Joe was physically dysfunctional.

Not only does dysfunction affect the whole family, it is also generational. I have a friend, a well-known lecturer, who says to audiences, "I'm sick of hearing about the dysfunctional family. Has anybody ever seen a functional family?" Her remark is usually met with laughter and applause. If we return to Joe's family, we see both the pervasiveness and the longitudinal aspect of dysfunction. Prior to Joe's accident, the family already had some rules, which solidified after the trauma of his accident. They were operating out of "don't feel," "don't talk," "don't ask for what you need," and "keep a stiff upper lip." As Joe's siblings left home and formed their own families, they tended to attach themselves to other needy people. The skills they had learned with Joe were easily transferable, and the dysfunctional pattern continued. Thus, the third and fourth generation became caretakers, all the while believing their family pattern was normal. After all, they never knew a time when it didn't exist. Therefore, it must be okay.

In an example I cited earlier in which a mother said to her children that "we don't cry in public," the children grew up with "we don't cry in public" operating like a badge of honor. It was a testimony of their strength. When I probed into this family rule with several of them, I discovered that "we don't cry in public" had translated to "we don't show what we are feeling to anyone, not even to each other." What had been a dubious point of pride earlier had become a massive dysfunction due to emotional repression in the present.

I think it is important to say something about the role of society in the development of dysfunction. Many of us believe that our problems stem from our families of origin and that if we could resolve those problems, we would be fine. If everybody resolved their family-of-origin problems, the world would be fine. I do not share this thinking. I believe that society itself operates with principles and norms that both support and foster dysfunction in individuals and in families.

My colleague Anne Wilson Schaef has written in her

ground-breaking book *When Society Becomes an Addict* that society actively supports addiction because, for many people, it is not possible to survive unless we are numbing ourselves to the pain of living in society as it presently operates.

Many of the institutions and organizations of society operate dysfunctionally. Consequently, you could conceivably have come from a healthy family only to find yourself immersed in dysfunction in your school or at work. In the experience of ACODs specifically, this fact can be a crucial issue. Many ACODs told me that, while their family's divorce was done in a healthy manner, the stigma and blame they experienced coming from their churches and schools left them feeling shamed and deficient. They carried shame for years, but it did not originate in their families.

Another way society fosters dysfunction is in the popular images it presents as symbols of normal relational life. Through most media, we are taught to expect marriages to be based on instant intimacy and families to resolve their issues easily within thirty-minute TV segments. We are bombarded with images that are completely unattainable in everyday life. It is not coincidental that addictions and dysfunctional families go hand in hand. Addictions give an artificial high and they block real feelings. There is a considerable amount of pain involved in living in a society that masks such dysfunction behind such a good-looking facade. No wonder relationships fail and divorce is so prevalent.

Understanding Divorce

So let us now turn to divorce. Technically speaking, divorce is the act that terminates a marriage contract and also terminates the existing family unit. It means "to sever," and indeed, in most divorces there is a distinct cutting off. Things change after divorce: relationships, living arrangements, finances, the number of persons in the family, etc. Nevertheless, the precise moment of divorce is rarely a major issue for ACODs. This is because divorce is more than the terminating of the marriage. Divorce is not just an event, it is a process.

The process of divorce has at least three phases. Phase one is the predivorce phase. This is the phase that leads up to the decision to terminate the marriage. For many ACODs, this is the period they remember when they look back on the divorce. For ACODs as children, this phase was marked by prolonged bickering, outright fighting, and a change in the family's usual routine. It is the period during which children felt that something was wrong, long before they had physical evidence that divorce was inevitable. In the predivorce phase, the parents exhibit a noticeable pulling away from one another, while the children experience a panic that something is happening that they cannot control.

My young friend Phil recognized the predivorce phase. He said, "Around the time I started high school, I knew something had changed between my parents. The only way I can describe it is that they stopped trying. Before this time I knew they had difficulties, but they seemed to want to resolve them. Suddenly, they didn't seem to have the energy for the marriage. They gave up."

Phase one, predivorce, is complex because often one parent wants the divorce and the other does not. Thus, unlike Phil's parents, one spouse is doubling his or her effort to save the marriage, while the other is resisting. Still, for most ACODs, the predivorce phase was a key point because the pain and trauma of this period is the ground from which sprang many of the feelings and behaviors that hamper them in adult life. For example, in the predivorce phase, many ACODs learned the "no talk rule." They sensed something was wrong in the family and with their parents, but they did not voice their fears. This behavior, continued in adulthood, is a burden to ACODs, who withhold speaking their needs in their intimate relationships.

The length of the predivorce phase should be examined. Given the complexity of the United States legal system, even an uncontested divorce can take a year or longer. When children are involved, the time is usually extended. On the average, the ACODs I spoke with went through a three-to-five-year predivorce period. For many others, predivorce lasted seven years or longer. Several remarked that they knew as young children that their parents' marriage was shaky, even though the actual separation came years later. So, we should be aware that there can be the "official" predivorce phase (which follows the parents' act of filing for divorce) and the "intuited" predivorce phase (when the child knows that divorce is a real possibility long before it is spoken about or acted upon by adults). I cite this difference because so many ACODs struggle with trusting their own perceptions. They trace their mistrust to the time when they sensed their parents were in trouble and were told they were mistaken or crazy.

The second phase of the divorce process is the divorce itself. Whereas the predivorce period is usually long and tedious, this second phase can be characterized by surprising rapidity. It is usually marked by the signing of divorce papers and/or appearing in court. ACODs remember coming home from school to find they would be moving elsewhere the next day, or if the family had already physically separated, they encountered one parent celebrating the divorce. As children, their response was quite different. They felt devastated. On the other hand, for many ACODs, the moment of divorce passed unnoticed. It merely confirmed what had been put into operation months or years earlier, i.e., the parents' separating physically, with one moving out of the family home.

Phase three, postseparation or postdivorce, can be as rocky as predivorce. Many ACODs felt especially vulnerable in this phase. They were shuttled between parents. They became little caretakers, especially when they felt one parent had been wronged. They were subjected to each parent's biases about the other. They acted as go-betweens and mediators, and many ACODs actually believed they could get their folks back together.

This phase, like predivorce, can be prolonged for years. In fact, for ACODs who have not resolved their issues arising out of their parents' divorce, this phase goes on throughout their lives. Even after parents are resolved in their feelings, children can continue in their efforts at reunion. They suffer needlessly. The oldest person in my survey, a sixty-two-year-old woman, confessed that she remained angry at her parents for divorcing until they died. She carried her anger with her into every gathering that included one of her parents, even though her parents were at peace with their decision. In this case, the ACOD kept the postdivorce phase alive, her parents did not. Of course, many parents remain hooked into their ex-spouses and frequently dump their hostilities on their children or complain bitterly about the "ex." All of these behaviors form the period of the postdivorce and affect children greatly.

I hope it is obvious from this discussion of the phases of divorce that when I write about adult children of divorce, I am referring to the process, not just the single decision to end a marriage. It is this long and drawn-out process that affects ACODs, not simply the fact of divorce.

Divorce, then, is not wrong or bad. Although some religious groups disagree with me, I am convinced divorce is not inherently dysfunctional. Divorce is a neutral event. *How* the divorce was carried out is the issue. The process of divorce is the single most important factor affecting ACODs.

Although divorce is neutral, it is still painful because of the dysfunction in the family, which affects the way the divorce is done. First, let's look at an example of divorce as the result of dysfunction in the family. In Phil's family, his mother was severely depressed. Consequently, she was listless and emotionally unavailable throughout most of Phil's life. Intellectually, Phil's father understood his wife's condition. However, he avoided his feelings about her depression by working hard and having several affairs. Within the household, no one ever spoke about how they felt. If you asked them, they would say "fine." Their denial of their feelings, their pretending to be normal, their acting "as if" Phil's mother was someone she wasn't, all contributed to their becoming farther out of touch with their reality as a family, and with each other. Intimacy was not possible at any level among them. In this case, the divorce was the result of prior dysfunction. Divorce was the symptom, along with other behaviors, that pointed to unhealthy processes that predated the divorce.

Often, people bring their unresolved emotional issues with them into marriage. Just as often, they marry believing that marriage will solve the problems. This is rarely the case. In fact, marriage usually exacerbates problems inherited from one's family of origin. Consequently, we should not make divorce the scapegoat, blaming it for issues that existed long before the marriage. Divorce is simply the inevitable outcome, the result, indeed just another symptom, of the underlying dysfunction.

Secondly, divorce can be done dysfunctionally. The entire three-phase process can be riddled with blaming, limitless anger, secrets, manipulation, and backstabbing. Feelings can be unacknowledged and never facilitated. Family members can feel battered by the process, and not free to be themselves. Not all divorces are executed in a dysfunctional manner. Later in this book, I describe divorces that were handled in a positive manner for all involved. Still, the dysfunctional process of divorce appears to be more prevalent, and it is my primary focus when I discuss ACOD issues in this book. This is due to the fact that many ACODs received powerful modeling as they witnessed their parents separate. Time after time, ACODs return to the lessons imprinted on their psyches by the process of divorce itself.

If we return to the umbrella concept of dysfunction, it is easy to see that for ACODs there are several ways to understand the effect of divorce. Most important for ACODs, the divorce process itself may have been the point where all the family's dysfunction intensified and was played out. As a result, ACODs find they must confront and heal from the ACOD characteristics described later in this book. Next, divorce may have been the result of previous dysfunction, and therefore the ACOD may have characteristics of an adult child of an alcoholic or otherwise addicted parent, along with ACOD issues. For example, the ACOD may have taken on one of the roles found in an alcoholic/addictive family such as the hero, scapegoat, lost child, or mascot, in addition to feeling such ACOD characteristics as helplessness, abandonment, taking sides, etc. Finally, in all dysfunction, we must remember society's role in promoting dysfunction. Even if, as children, we came through our family experiences relatively unscathed, we can still be affected by the dysfunction in society and its institutions.

Divorce can be one form of dysfunction that coexists with other forms of dysfunction and is interrelated with them. However, divorce is unusual and different from other dysfunction in that divorce often stops a dysfunctional situation between parents, while continuing a dysfunctional situation for children. Parents seek and usually find relief after divorce, whereas some children feel more burdened. Thus, divorce is a mixed blessing and a complex phenomenon. Other forms of dysfunction certainly affect the family. However, divorce is one of the few processes that actually terminates an existing family unit. In this, divorce goes beyond other forms of dysfunction. The ending of the family as the child knows it is the power of divorce. This is also unique to divorce, and the reason the effects of divorce are so deeply embedded in the lives of ACODs. There are many issues that, for ACODs, flow from the ending of the family unit. The ways that ACODs coped with these issues are explored in the characteristics of ACODs that follow later in this book.

Having looked at the interrelationship of divorce and dysfunction, I want to move on to a fuller description of addiction and abuse. Both of these issues are heard in the stories of ACODs, and they give a particular set of problems to the divorce process, as well as to adult-child adjustment. After a look at the effect of addictions and abuse on ACODs, I will focus on divorce itself, and the feelings and behaviors ACODs carry as a result of how divorce was experienced in their families.

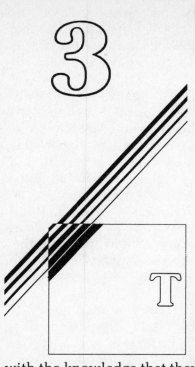

Addiction and the ACOD

T he ACODs whose parents' divorce was the result of addiction, or where addiction exacerbated the process, can console themselves with the knowledge that they are not alone. Indeed, addictions are epidemic in our society. One commentator, Sharon Wegscheider-Cruse, estimates that 96 percent of the population comes from families in which addiction played a role in family dysfunction.[1] Although Wegscheider-Cruse's statistics are alarming, they point to the pervasiveness of addictions in the society and to the intergenerational aspect of the addictive disease. If addictions are not intervened upon, they do continue from generation to generation. Why are addictions such an issue for divorcing families? I believe addictions take over the life process in the divorcing family. They are all-consuming, and they are, by definition, a family disease.

Addictions Are All-Consuming

Traditionally, we believed that persons were addicted solely to substances. The most well-known addictive substances are alcohol, drugs, and food. Over the past ten years it has become obvious that in addition to the substance addictions, there are also process addictions. The most common process addictions are work, spending, gambling, debting, sex, relationships, and religion. Increasingly, there is evidence that any process can be used addictively.

The paradigm of addiction is the same regardless of whether the addiction is to a substance such as food or a process such as relationships. When people are practicing their addiction, their life becomes increasingly unmanageable. Basically, this means that the addiction is in control of you, you are no longer in charge of yourself or your addictive behavior. You are incapable of saying no. Addictions, then, are chronic, progressive, and fatal. Fifty years of research on addictions has shown that addictions do not go away by spontaneous remission. If you do not actively interrupt them, they inevitably end in death. Those who are actively involved in their addictions die on many levels—spiritually, emotionally, mentally, and physically.

Addictions are all-consuming in that they keep the addict busy. You are always thinking about the addiction, looking forward to the next "hit," protecting your stash or supply from those who may be concerned about you. Addictions take you away from your own feelings and consequently away from loved ones. An addiction will always take the edge off feelings; it puts a buffer between yourself and your awareness. Addictions keep you from being present to what is going on around you. It is nearly impossible to relate to an addict because the person is "not home," he is taken over by the addiction.

As information about addiction has grown, it has become commonly accepted that most addicts must deal with more than one addiction. This fact will be obvious to anyone who has ever attended an Alcoholics Anonymous meeting, only to find himself in a room filled with smoke and coffee cups. It is not unusual to have a cluster of addictions. For example, a work addict may also use food addictively. The food addiction is a way of taking the edge off the pain of excessive working.

All of the individual addictions share an underlying addictive process. The addictive process is characterized by denial, dishonesty, control, self-centeredness, grandiosity, thinking processes that are compulsive, dualistic, and overly rational and logical. All addictions end with ethical deterioration and the loss of spirituality.

Early in recovery, the addict deals with the specific addiction (for example, the addiction to alcohol). The craving for alcohol is not an issue throughout life. The challenge is to not get triggered into the "disease," which means entering into the above characteristics. This is one of the reasons recovering addicts wisely say they are always recovering, never recovered, for who among us can deal with our dishonesty or our judgmentalism once and for all?

Many families come apart because they cannot withstand the pressure and daily craziness of the addictive process. Unfortunately, it is not just the addict who has a disease where addictions are involved. The family suffers, too, but not as victims. They are also participants.

A Family Disease

Formerly, family members believed the addict had a problem. We now recognize that the addict has a treatable disease. We previously thought the family suffered *from* the addict's disease. We now see that addiction *is* a family disease. Every family member is affected by the addict's disease. Usually, family members participate in the addictive process by becoming hooked on the troubles of the addict, attempting to control the addict, or by rescuing and caretaking of the addict. These behaviors, which have been called codependent, are dysfunctional for each family member. For the family to be anything but dysfunctional, each family member must begin a program of recovery, right alongside the addict.

As our knowledge of addictions grows, we have learned that entire families must face their addictive process. Usually the primary addict is identified first. Later, the spouse acknowledges codependency or relationship addiction (he or she is addicted to the partner and cannot conceive of life without that person). A child may be an overeater (nourishing himself with food in the absence of other nurturing), another child may become a workaholic (using work to avoid intimacy and deaden the pain of family dysfunction). Whatever form the addictive process takes, it spreads in an almost contagious manner in families.

Both the prevalence of addictions and the involvement of families in addictions are critical issues in the divorce process. In my interviews with ACODs, addictions figured prominently in 80 percent of their stories. This means that 80 percent of the ACODs in my study were dealing with both the stress of the divorce and the stress of the addiction. In most of these cases, the dysfunction in the family is attributable to the addiction. Certainly, the addictive process had a great impact upon how the divorce process itself was carried out.

The dysfunction of divorce and the addictive process have many things in common. In the dysfunctional divorce, adults *blame* each other. They rarely accept responsibility for things they might have done. In the addictive process, the addict also blames. Through shifting blame to someone else, the addict keeps the focus off his or her disease.

The addictive process is characterized by *isolation* and pulling away from support and/or confrontation. Addicts isolate themselves to protect their stash. Family and friends pull away in denial, confusion, and embarrassment. In the dysfunctional divorce, the family retreats into itself and does not show that it needs help. Family members feel ashamed and keep their internal troubles to themselves. Moreover, as Wallerstein and Blakeslee point out in *Second Chances*, divorce is the only major family crisis in which social supports fall away. Neither the church, neighbors, nor social clubs will rally around to assist a divorcing family. The family finds itself more alone.

The addictive process is permeated with *denial*. No one lets him or herself see what is really going on. The dysfunctional divorce thrives on denial. In many cases, ACODs were told to deny their perceptions about their parents' relationships. An ACOD who, as a young child of eight, witnessed her father attack her mother was told by her father, "You didn't see that."

The dysfunctional family experienced *perfectionism* that turned sour. Many ACODs came from families where mothers tried to be perfect homemakers and wives. They poured their thwarted ambitions into activities they thought would please, and still they found themselves without a spouse and without marketable skills. Every addict confronts perfectionism in the form of the belief that it is not acceptable to be human like others. The illusion that it is possible to be godlike dies slowly with addicts.

As children of divorce, ACODs found themselves taking sides, feeling torn with conflicting loyalties to their parents. The addictive process thrives on *dualism*. In dualistic thinking, we go back and forth between two sides or black-and-white options, with the belief that we can figure out what is right. We have no understanding of the middle ground, or "gray" issues or people. We believe all we have to do is get on the right side and we will be justified. Finding the right side is a process that tormented many ACODs as children. In the most dysfunctional divorces, parents supported the competition. There was no neutrality. The addictive system is a closed system, and dualism keeps the system closed, just as ACODs' futile attempts at side-taking did in their families. ACODs stayed so busy with "sides," they didn't perceive that they had needs, and that their needs may have had nothing to do with their parents.

Addicts are thoroughly *self-centered*. They interpret everything as happening for or against them, and they will do anything to get their fix. The dysfunctional divorce felt very self-centered to the ACODs. There seemed to be no support for them. They felt alone as their parents pursued their process and became intensely involved in conflict resolution. Children felt bereft and left out, as if they did not matter.

In the dysfunctional divorce, attempts at *control* are common. Children witnessed their parents vying for control of finances, property, and custody. Parents rarely spoke directly to one another about their wishes. Lawyers entered the process and compounded the control problem. ACODs remember trying to get control of their feelings because their feelings would only add to the burden on the family. The addictive process is built on control, or the illusion of control. Addicts believe they can control their compulsive behavior. They believe they can control how others see them. This is part of their grandiosity. The paradox of recovery is that as soon as addicts admit powerlessness and the loss of control over the addiction, that is the moment at which their recovery begins and they are able to stop using.

In the addictive system, the codependent says, "I can handle this myself. I'll do it alone." The children of divorce believe they need to do it alone, too. They have experienced loss of intimate support and they feel alone. They are often ashamed to reach out and share with others, not wanting to feel different from their peers. So, they "go it alone," usually taking on more than they can handle, assuming burdens not meant for children.

The addict is always making *promises* that are never kept. This is part of the dishonesty and conning of the addictive process. The addict frequently promises things she cannot possibly carry out. Sometimes the addict forgets the promise due to memory loss, an effect of the addiction. Often, the promise is made to get someone off the addict's back and is promptly forgotten. ACODs feel that many promises were broken. In the heat of the divorce and after it, parents made promises that were intended to distract children from the pain of divorce. Some of these promises were unthinkingly made and could not be carried out. A majority of promises were broken. Vacations were promised, as were gifts. Several ACODs remember being promised a pet after the divorce was finalized. The newly single parent then realized that a pet only added to the tension of an already stressful lifestyle, and conveniently forgot or put off the promise. ACODs began to wonder if their parents could be trusted. Some felt dangerously alone with someone who did not keep promises.

These are just some of the similar characteristics shared by the addictive process and the divorce process. In families where there were active addicts, the families became so enmeshed with the addict as well as with one another that it was nearly impossible for children to have a life separate from the troubles of the family. This sense of being overwhelmed by the process of divorce is also common in ACODs' stories.

It is interesting to note that substance abuse is prevalent in the parents of ACODs, while process addictions are predominant in the lives of the ACODs themselves. According to my study, in the families of origin of the ACODs the majority of addicted fathers are described as alcoholic. Some combined alcohol and marijuana. Some mothers are also described as alcoholic, but primarily they became codependent with the alcoholic husband.

Here is a story typical of many ACODs. It was told to me by Jack, who was fifteen when his parents divorced.

My father was a banker, and I suppose he was a workaholic because he worked constantly, even on vacations. But the thing he did every weekend was drink enormous amounts. He would start with beer and move on to bourbon. Then he would get into his rage. He tore up the house so many times it is a wonder we had a place to live. After a rage, he would take off, only to return in the early hours of the morning, full of remorse. This behavior went on for twelve years, and it was constant except on holidays, when Dad's own parents were around. Because he was a binge drinker, and he appeared to be able to control it, Mom denied he was alcoholic. She put up with the weekend rages, although she became more depressed as the years went on. She finally filed for a divorce after a particularly violent weekend when he pulled all her china and crystal out of the cabinet. The next day he couldn't remember anything.

Jack sees his father regularly and says the binges have decreased somewhat since the divorce, but alcoholism is still a problem for his father. Jack describes himself as a relationship addict—a person who attaches to other people and their problems and cannot live without them. He bears a striking resemblance to other ACODs in his preference for process addictions.

Here is the range of addictions that ACODs told me they deal with at this time in their lives:

Workaholism

"It keeps me busy and not feeling my pain. Also, constantly thinking about work, even during my leisure time, keeps me from addressing my intimacy needs. I throw myself into work without consideration of my health needs or the needs of others."

Spending/Debting

"Every chance I get, I buy stuff for myself. These are all things that are not necessities for my life. I feel I can't get enough and I pamper myself in ways that are selfish. My spending deprives my family of things they need. I had such a rotten childhood, I feel I owe it to myself."

Thinking

"My thinking processes are about to ruin my life. I exhaust myself with compulsive thinking. I try to figure everything out. My mind is questioning, examining, all I do. I am never sure, never unsure. I believe I can think my way to a resolution of my parents' divorce and I can think my way to happiness. I want a logical, rational answer to everything. My thinking blocks me from feeling, and thus, I keep the illusion of control. Unfortunately, it is exhausting. My addiction is invisible. You can't see me doing it, but I am, all the time."

Food/Coffee/Sugar

"I use binge eating to avoid facing my painful feelings. Also, I use coffee and sugar because I am afraid of fatigue and tiredness. It is too much like the hopeless boredom of my family."

Religion

"I sought the church as a haven of community after my parents' split. I hoped religion would do for me what my family wouldn't—give me safety and some answers about life. I am obsessed with religion to the point that I have lost my own spirituality. I use religion to avoid finding my own answers to life's deepest questions. I will not make any major decision without absolute guidance from religion."

Drugs/Alcohol

"I dealt with my unhappy family situation by using drugs and alcohol, beginning at age thirteen. It numbed the loneliness I felt and I thought I could quit anytime. Actually, during the divorce process, my folks had less time for me so my use went unnoticed, I thought. By sixteen, I was hooked and my father put me in treatment. As an adult, I still use drugs and alcohol whenever I feel anxious or to put down a strong feeling."

Most ACODs began their involvement with the addictive process in their late teens, or at least that is when they became aware of it. The addiction served to block out some of the pain as they began the developmental challenges of adolescence without the nurturing support of two parents. Combined with the above addictions, relationships, sex, and romance addictions are found in great numbers of ACODs' stories.

Relationship, Sex, and Romance Addictions

Escape From Intimacy, by Anne Wilson Schaef, describes the forms of the "pseudorelationship" addictions, which she says have nothing to do with love. They are addictive relationships in which a person is either (1) addicted to a particular person and that person's problems, or (2) the person is in a relationship simply because he or she cannot conceive of the possibility of *not* being in a relationship, or (3) the person fantasizes relationships with inappropriate people, e.g., the teenage cashier at the grocery store. The relationship addict goes from one relationship to another, often less concerned about a particular partner than the pursuit of the high of the relationship itself.

Then there are the sex addictions, which include sexual fantasies, acting out sexually, sexual abuse, excessive masturbation, pornography, and sexual anorexia.

Finally, Schaef describes romance addictions, which include the addiction to causes, and the refusal to see people and situations for what they really are because of an attachment to the "romance" surrounding them. Romance addicts get hooked on faraway places, candlelight, and appearances. They are not interested in the substance of a relationship, but in how it looks. They create a look and a fantasy and try to live in it, rather than being real.[2]

ACODs seem to specialize in the relationship, sex, and romance addictions. Their stories are full of instances of obsessive relationships. Karl came to see me two years after his parents' separation. He described himself as a "jock," someone who excelled in sports and who had gone through life relatively problem free. I had seen Karl in other settings and would agree with his description of himself. However, on the day of our talk, Karl seemed uncharacteristically sad. Karl's mother left the family when he was twenty-one. Karl says he was shaken by her disappearance, even though he was supposedly grown-up. "I really began to question my ability to form lasting relationships. My world was shaken, and I doubted everything I had previously believed."

Karl went through a series of girlfriends after his parents' divorce. His predominant feeling was fear of not having someone in his life he could be intimate with, yet he hardly stayed with anyone long enough to develop true intimacy. Moreover, Karl confided to me that he used the high he got from relationships to avoid the pain of his fear. In this he shows Schaef's second form of relationship addiction in that he uses relationships to escape facing himself. Karl soon came to see that most of the women he dated were merely objects. His main issue was fear of being alone. Who the young women were was secondary. In some cases, he was not even compatible with them. During our visit, Karl said to me, "I never want to feel the fear and loneliness I suffered after Mom left. I'm terrified of being alone."

Some ACODs block intimacy with multiple relationships (you feel close, but you are not), while other ACODs avoid intimacy through fear and sexual anorexia. Lorrie combined sexual anorexia with excessive caretaking of others (also a form of relationship addiction). Lorrie's mother dealt with her divorce by becoming addicted to soap operas. As the family was coming apart, she immersed herself in more soaps, blurring the boundaries between the fantasy world on television and her own situation. "I think my mother wanted to believe that what was happening to her was really a drama. She used phrases like 'I can't believe this divorce is happening to me. I feel like I'm watching a soap on TV.' It was frightening to lose both my father—he moved out—and my mother—she moved into a fantasy world."

Lorrie says she is obsessed with thinking about sex, but she is fearful of sexual involvement. She avoids all encounters that may lead to sexual activity, yet her life is ruled by thoughts of sex. She relates to people through excessive giving and caretaking. She often controls other people with her niceness. Lorrie pondered her sexual addiction. She said she was determined not to be like her mother, who lived in a fantasy world. Yet, as she reviewed her life, she saw that her sexual anorexia and her fantasizing had resulted in her being very much like her mother. Lorrie used a fantasy world to remove herself from reality and the possibilities of intimacy, and her life was much the same as her mother's was in her divorcing family.

During the divorce process, many ACODs witnessed a disturbing level of partying and sexual activity. An ACOD whose mother took her on dates says, "My first date was at age nine, when my mother began taking me out with her and her boyfriend. I guess you could say I got my sex education beginning then." Several ACODs recall with embarrassment that their parents began acting like teenagers, throwing wild parties and confiding in them like a friend. "At a time in my life when I needed a parent, I got a thirty-five-year-old best friend, sharing things with me I barely understood. It was scary. I felt close to my mom, but I didn't feel like she was a mom anymore." This scenario was related by a twenty-nine-year-old ACOD who said she had trouble maintaining clear boundaries between herself and others. Her sexual addiction took the form of getting sexually involved very quickly with people, then breaking off the relationship when it was clear they had little in common, which happened repeatedly.

Finally, we need to consider the role of romance addiction in the divorcing families, and in the lives of ACODs themselves. Family-of-origin stories from ACODs are filled with tales of parents who played at being parents with a woeful lack of preparation. Marriages seem to have been built on instant intimacy, and when that facade crumbled, there was nothing substantial holding the partners together. Impression management was the order of the day, as middle-class suburban families bought the right car, had the right dog, and wore the right clothes. ACOD families looked outside themselves for models of family life. The few they found were hollow. Families floundered under modern stress, addictions grew, and marriages came apart in record numbers.

Charlene is one of many examples of an ACOD whose romance addiction began in her family of origin. The older of two children, she describes her family as "picture-book." She says, "My family was not just influenced by advertising and popular trends. We *were* the trends. My mother dressed us in the latest fashions. We bought furniture that was 'in' and changed it with every new wave. We looked like we had emerged from a magazine. My family was not particularly religious—we never went to church—but my father picked up that prayer was something that good families did, so we started every meal with grace. We were fluff on the outside. We imitated ideal parents and their children in our interactions by feigning closeness that simply did not exist. We also compared ourselves to other families, usually with the result that the others couldn't measure up to us. We felt superior and we liked to be noticed."

Charlene's romance addiction was fostered at an early age because her family was more interested in how they appeared than in how they felt. They lived an illusion that their romantic view of themselves would carry them through any adversity, thus avoiding the daily work of relating to one another.

The idealized, romantic notion of family grew sour when Charlene's father revealed he had been seeing another woman and he wanted a divorce. "It was a shock to me that my perfect father had a secret life," said Charlene. "I simply could not put the two together, so I created a romantic fantasy about this being my father's 'true love.' It was all a lie, of course. But it showed me how invested I was in keeping up appearances."

As an ACOD, Charlene becomes overly involved in good causes with downtrodden people. She frequently idealizes them as faultless, excuses their behavior, and refuses to see them for who they are, a carryover from the romanticizing she learned in her family.

Like Charlene, the children of these severed unions, ACODs, move into their own relationships and perpetuate the romance addiction. They believe there is a perfect mate out there for them. They see marriage as a haven where, for once, "I'll do it right." They dress for success and work like dogs, all in the service of creating pseudorelationships where people won't get too close. They are surrounded by increasingly slicker, more seductive advertising, and tunes on the radio pumping out addictive love song lyrics that tell them they can't survive without having that love object. Their physical senses and their sense of themselves are numbed by every addiction known to humankind. They began adulthood with few models of healthy relationships. Is it any wonder that romance addiction is the addiction of choice among ACODs?

Divorce and Addiction

Divorce and addiction are related in that addiction sets up the circumstances under which a healthy family life is not possible. All addictions separate family members from each other because the addictive process in the family and in the individual is so all-consuming that there is little opportunity for self-care or attending to the family's own process. Even as the addictive process dulls the pain of the individual addict, it paradoxically throws the family into chaos and into more pain.

Addiction frequently causes divorce because eventually one of the partners decides that he or she cannot put up with the craziness of the addiction any longer. To survive, you separate. As they separated, many parents forgot that in leaving the addicted spouse they did not escape the addictive process. The addictive process comes with the family members into their next family unit, and into their subsequent relationships. This is what it means to be an adult child. You carry into your future the dysfunctional roles you practiced in your family of origin. You live by the rules you learned there, even though those rules are no longer needed.

Consequently, ACODs are affected by two processes when addiction figured prominently in their parents' decision to divorce. They have the issues of adult children of addiction (ACOA), and they may be addicted themselves. Then, in the divorce, ACODs experienced the ending of their family of origin, with its particular problems and feelings. Even when the family unit was severely troubled, the divorce was a kind of death, a true loss. For some ACODs, getting away from an addicted parent may be a relief, but it does not end the problems the ACOD must face. There are still ambivalent feelings about that parent, and losing the first family you knew is never easy. ACOD healing, to be complete, needs to encompass healing from the pain of addiction and the trauma of divorce.

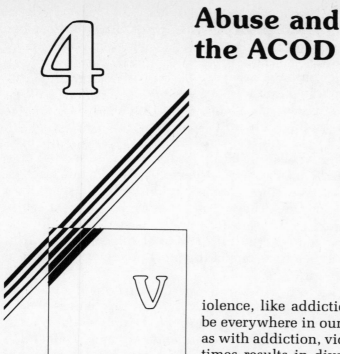

Abuse and the ACOD

4

iolence, like addiction, seems to be everywhere in our society, and as with addiction, violence sometimes results in divorce. Indeed, divorcing families tend to be filled with violence. For our purposes, I am defining violence and abuse as any act (physical, verbal, or psychological) by which one person deliberately injures another, and his or her welfare is threatened or harmed. Statistics on the occurrence of wife, husband, and child abuse are hard to gather since many batterers do not admit to their acts. The same is true of the abused. An American Association for Protecting Children report documented 1,726,649 cases of abused and neglected children in 1984. Wife abuse was placed at 30 per 1,000 women in 1985.[1]

In my ACOD survey, about 40 percent of all respondents had witnessed physical violence, listened to verbal abuse, or experienced sexual abuse by a family member. Sometimes the violence occurred during the point of highest stress for the parents. More typically, violence was a way of life, the accepted way of handling things in the family. No one factor seems to explain the causes of violence in the divorcing family, and there are certain patterns in the stories of ACODs.

The Stressful Circumstances Surrounding the Divorce

Divorcing parents are under tremendous stress. Ordinarily, people look to their partners and to those they know intimately for assistance during stress. In divorce, the very person you thought you could count on, your spouse, is the person from whom you feel most estranged. Thus, your first source of stress arises out of a sense of unsafeness with the spouse you had once trusted. In the violent family, this issue is exacerbated because some spouses are in daily physical danger from their partner. They never know when the next eruption will occur, so they are in a constant state of readiness. Stress-management charts put divorce at the top of the list, second only to death, as one of the most taxing experiences a human can endure.

In addition to the loss of the partner and the disillusionment with the relationship, divorce, like death, changes nearly all other aspects of life. Divorcing parents are changing their residences, their financial arrangements, and their relationship to their children. In families where income is lower, stress is higher. Overall, during the time when the parents and children are most in need of the support of familiar surroundings and emotional stability, they are least available. It is under these kinds of circumstances that violence is most likely to erupt.

Violent Parents Were Frequently Abused as Children

There have been many studies that have questioned whether abusive parents were themselves abused. Although the evidence is not conclusive, it does appear that parents are powerful models even when we know that their behavior is wrong. Thus, over the generations, children tend to act out their parents' dysfunctional behaviors.

People who experienced violence in their homes say they use violence when they know of nothing else to do. Thalia's story is typical of many I heard in my interviews with ACODs.

Thalia is a therapist who works for a social service agency. She says she was attracted to therapy as a profession because her own life was one of struggle and violence. She wants to help others, although lately she finds herself feeling resentful of her clients. When I observed that perhaps she had not finished her own process around her divorcing family, her eyes immediately filled with tears. "I think you may be right," she said, sniffing. "I feel so angry just thinking about my family, especially my mother." Thalia went on to describe her mother's family, rural Southern farmers. "There was never enough money in my grandmother's house. Grandpa took off when the last of five children was born. Grandma's usual way of getting my mother and my uncles to work around the farm was through threats of beatings. She grumbled about the kids being shiftless and lazy, and my mother was frequently beaten. Her left arm is disfigured from a severe burn she received during one of my grandmother's rages when she pushed my mother into a wood-burning stove." Thalia paused. She seemed to be in another world. Her tears were flowing steadily, and I waited with her to see where she would go with her memories. "I knew my mother hated the treatment she received at home, and she got out of there the first thing she could. I also know, at least I want to believe, that Grandma was not an evil person. I think she felt powerless and she took it out on the kids. Still, it hurts to think of how scared those kids must have been." As Thalia described her mother's childhood, I wondered if her tears were for herself, for her own story is equally horrendous.

Thalia's mother divorced when Thalia was three. The cycle of poverty that had begun on the farm continued when Thalia's mother moved to the city. She was a teenage mother who was unskilled for most jobs, so she lived on welfare and an occasional support check from Thalia's father. "I recall watching my mother's anger rise as the days went by without a support check from Dad. She tried everything. She called him, she threatened. When nothing worked with my father, I knew to get out of the way. The anger was coming at me, next." Thalia was slapped, kicked, and verbally berated by her mother for four years after the divorce. She subsequently ran away and sought protection from the court.

There was a long silence in the room after Thalia finished

her story. She had been crying throughout it, and I was struck with the similarity of the grandmother and the mother: poverty, single parenting under the worst circumstances, powerlessness that gets taken out on kids. "Sure, I cry for myself," Thalia said, "but I cry for all of us, Grandma, Mom, me. We just did things we knew were wrong and didn't work, but we couldn't seem to help ourselves."

Divorcing Families Are Isolated

The most violent stories come from situations where no one else is watching. Many divorcing families turn in on themselves. They neither seek outside help, nor is it offered. The nuclear family is already a little island unto itself, but the divorcing family is more so. Relatives are usually at a distance. As the divorce proceeds, no one wants to meddle. The family is left to handle its own dysfunctional process. These days, divorcing parents seek marriage counseling. Fifteen or twenty years ago, it was less common. An ACOD attests to her isolation in her story: "My father split when I was in high school. I went between two worlds. In school, I played strong. I said I was fine. I didn't share what was going on at home. I was so ashamed. I never invited anyone home, it was so unpredictable. Before my father left, I never knew if they'd be fighting. After he left, Mom fought with him over the phone." In this family, the fighting escalated from verbal to physical battering, but there were no witnesses and the children remained silent, not seeking help from school authorities.

Although there is evidence that the stress of lowered income results in increased battering, we should not be naive enough to believe that abuse does not cut across all economic levels. Violence erupts in the "best" of families.

For the ACOD, observing and experiencing violence teaches some very specific things. These three lessons come from Gelles and Straus's work on intimate violence. They contend that observing your parents hit one another is more likely to result in your becoming a violent adult than if you were hit yourself. You learn that:

1. Those who love you are also those who hit you, and those you love are people you can hit.

2. Seeing and experiencing violence in your home establishes the moral rightness of hitting those you love.
3. If other means of getting your way, dealing with stress, or expressing yourself do not work, violence is permissible.[2]

These are powerful lessons and many ACODs learned them well. As we will see later in the characteristics, ACODs confuse fighting with intimacy. One young man confirmed this in describing his own history. "I knew beating up on people was wrong, but fighting was such a way of life at our house that, as I grew older, I just fell into shouting and threatening more and more. New behaviors felt awkward, and I usually get what I want from shouting, so I keep using it."

Growing up around violence resulted in some ACODs' having many personal problems. They did poorly in school, they tangled with their peers, they had trouble making friends, they started drinking and drugging early in adolescence. ACODs felt worthless and fearful. And they fought with others and with family members. They did not trust adults. The first adults in their lives, their parents, inflicted violent unhappiness on them, and they felt abandoned by them.

Several ACODs discussed the effect of violence on their schooling. They said that as the family disintegrated, it was almost impossible to concentrate at school. They were physically exhausted from the tension at home. Homework went unfinished and they daydreamed in class. When the violence was spread over years, these children's scores on standardized intelligence tests dropped. Most troublesome of all, their aggressiveness grew. This vignette from a thirty-three-year-old ACOD man is a poignant reminder of the effects of violence.

It is a miracle I am even functional today. My father beat my mother regularly, and I was abused by both of them. By the time I got to school, I was so wary of adults I wouldn't let anyone touch me. In first grade, when a teacher tried to help me with my jacket, I ran from her. I was a troublemaker all through school. I guess you'd say I was a delinquent. It took six years for my mother to leave my dad. She didn't beat on me as I got older. I was too big and she knew I could beat her up if I wanted. But she continued the verbal abuse. I am saddest about the fact that I was surrounded by adults who could have helped me, but I couldn't distinguish between them and my crazy, abusive family. I pushed everyone away with my own aggression. That is the tragedy of violence. You feel so alone!

Some ACODs were utterly alone in the violent home, and they insulated themselves, out of fear, from intervention by those who could have helped. Those who seemed to escape the long-term effects of violence were those who found a protective, nurturing adult. I love Joe's story. It shows the importance of extended family and a strong grandmother!

Joe, an exuberant twenty-eight-year-old, was one who survived with minimal long-term damage. Joe was physically abused by his father, whose rage escalated during the divorce proceedings. Joe also observed his mother and father in arguments that ended in punching and kicking. But the tide turned when Joe's grandmother arrived on the scene. She took one look at the situation and bundled Joe and his sister into her car and took them to her home "until the troubles are over." Although the children eventually lived full-time with their mother, Joe felt he had a haven of safety with his grandmother and he returned there often. Today, he appears to have come through a violent, divorcing family relatively unscathed.

The ACODs who experienced violence and abuse as children reach adulthood with some very specific issues. As ACODs, they usually need to deal directly with one or all of the following:

ACODs Must Deal with Their Aggression

ACODs learned that fighting and violence were acceptable and now they use them. Aggression is not acceptable, nor is it appropriate as a means of relating and communicating. It may feel familiar, but that does not make aggression normal as a way of getting what one wants.

ACODs Believe Intimacy Means Fighting

ACODs confuse fighting with closeness. If they shut down emotionally during their parents' divorce, fighting may be the only thing that enables them to feel. Still, ACODs are not necessarily close with another when they fight. They may risk anger with those they really care for, yet they should not confuse real connecting with fighting. They are not the same.

ACODs Must Learn to Establish Appropriate Boundaries

The problem with violence is that it is like a river out of its banks, or more exactly, like a tidal wave. Violence tends to suck everything and everyone into its vortex. It flows out over everything. The divorce process, which itself seems to take over the family's life, is greatly exacerbated by the introduction of violence. ACODs emerge from these traumas with a lowered sense of themselves and confusion about limits. For example, some ACODs may not know that it is not appropriate to walk into a room without knocking. People were always walking in on them. A closed door was no barrier. Some may not know that certain kinds of touching are wrong, for ACODs were touched in those ways. Much of what happened to ACODs was disrespectful of their boundaries, and they cannot count on their experience to be the standard for how to act.

ACODs Must Confront Their Fear of Change

As a defense against the unpredictability of violence, ACODs became very rigid about change. Change was usually sprung on them without preparation. They go to extremes to guard against its surprise. When presented with change, ACODs overreact. They never change plans without a lot of preparation. Their control needs are excessive in relation to change. This attitude can debilitate them in their personal lives and in their jobs. The world is in process and change is constant. ACODs become locked into rigidity, a rigidity that is no longer needed.

ACODs Need to Give Themselves Time, Space, and Support for Healing from Sexual Abuse

Incest is a form of intimate violence. It encompasses all of the earlier issues of change, boundaries, intimacy, and aggression. However, incest was usually secret, so ACODs may feel especially alone in dealing with it. Also, parents often deny that their children were incested, which encourages the children themselves to mistrust their own memories or bodily sensations. As children, ACODs may have repressed the memories of their incest. Only as adults do they begin to get glimmers of their past. Healing from incest is an essential process. It is separate from ACOD recovery, which usually focuses on the effect of divorce. It takes time and a safe environment. ACODs may find that intimacy with a partner is not possible until they work through incest issues. Sexual abuse is not solely a women's issue. Men are sexually abused, also.

It is the experience of many sexually abused ACODs that until they are in a safe environment, they cannot deal with their feelings about the sexual abuse. Since separating families were not safe, incest issues rarely came up until ACODs were out of their families. Consequently, they reach their thirties and forties before they first confront the effects of early sexual abuse. Healing from sexual abuse is a major task, sometimes taking years. It is an essential process within the larger process of putting their lives back together.

Violence has many forms in the divorcing family. Some of the most destructive forms, e.g., incest, are the least obvious. Whether the violence was sexual, physical, verbal, or psychological, it had the effect of pushing the family into dysfunction and ultimately into divorce. Again, it is important to realize that divorce does not cause violence. Violence is a choice. That parents keep resorting to violence indicates that dysfunction is already present. Divorce doesn't "make" people violent. For ACODs, violence has a legacy. Some ACODs acquired dysfunctional patterns of relating by witnessing violence. Relearning appropriate ways of relating is a task that ACODs must take on to heal from the effects of violence-ridden divorce.

As I was researching the long-term effects of divorce on ACODS, I had the opportunity to try my ideas out on several audiences. I always welcomed these interactions, as each group inevitably contained many ACODs who had lots to say about my findings. Most ACODs reacted with relief that someone was recognizing their experience; many were animated in lending their stories and comparing their families with others. But when it came to the effects of addiction and violence on the divorce process, I was often met with anger. ACODs whose families split from addiction-induced divorces or divorces that were fraught with violence felt especially burdened and resentful about their pasts. Larry is an example of many I met.

Larry is furious. I can see his anger rising through his body and into his face. He is almost incoherent, his words stumbling out. "It's not fair!" he says. "I have enough to deal with coming from a divorced family. Why do I have to deal with all this other stuff like violence and addictions?" Larry, who is thirty-two, is just now letting himself remember his family history, which included several severe beatings by an alcoholic father.

Larry is right. It seems a double-barreled oppression to find oneself victimized by divorce as well as violence and addiction. As we will see later, not all divorces are as dysfunctional as the one Larry experienced in his family, yet an alarming amount of violence often accompanies divorce. Enough to ask, "What is going on in our society that we have generations of adults bringing so much dysfunction into the new families they start?"

Although Larry believes he is one of a kind, his companions are legion. He will have the task of grieving over his past, taking responsibility for his current behavior, and hopefully passing on his learning to his children. But Larry cannot be alone in this task. As a society, we have to be shocked into action in the face of the damage now being visited upon children. Until we examine and change the social system that puts such pressure on families, we will continue to perpetuate dysfunction, and we will have a very difficult future.

Types of Divorce

5

I have been discussing the effects of divorce as it is interrelated with addiction and abuse. It is important to do this because divorce is not just a single issue in the lives of ACODs. When divorce comes encumbered by addiction and abuse, it can feel as if there are several strands to sort out. Or as one young man joked, "I know I got a mess a trouble. My family was like an octopus, all legs going at once!"

I want to turn now to divorce itself: the process of divorce and the fact of divorce. For ACODs, divorce is the center of the octopus. Sure, all the tentacles are moving, but for the ACOD those tentacles are connected back to the center of the creature and that center is called divorce. Divorce was a primary feature of ACOD family experience, an event both traumatic and long lasting and one that was influential in the formation of their personalities, their relationships, even the way they perform a job.

Age at the Time of Divorce

Before we move to a consideration of the types of divorce, I want to reflect on whether age at the time ACODs went through their family's breakup has any bearing on the long-term effects of the experience. There is not much known about age at the time the divorce took place in relation to postdivorce development. What is written is tentative. A *Scientific American* study contends divorce is hardest on adolescents, for they find themselves without a role model at a time of sexual maturation, and they may experience a deep sense of abandonment.[1]

Wallerstein and Blakeslee, in *Second Chances*, believe that divorce is easiest on preschool children. When there are older siblings, they give the very young child extra protection. These little children have only vague memories of the parent who leaves, and no entrenched memories of the intact family. They cannot hearken back to "the way it was" and so do not feel the loss of the former family as intensely as the older child.[2]

I asked my respondents to tell me how they felt at the time of the divorce. I also asked them to describe the issues they now deal with as adults. I do not believe that any identifiable pattern emerges out of their descriptions, and yet they do carry some interesting themes. These are described below.

Preschool: Ages 1–5

As one would expect, preschoolers remember little about divorce. They were too young, or they didn't understand what was happening. Their needs were simple enough and they experienced things like wanting "Daddy to tuck me in bed at night like he always did."

Three- and four-year-olds had feelings they remember. Several male ACODs say they felt alone, "like my father had left because of me, because he did not love me anymore." Other three- and four-year-olds felt guilty and crushed and "like I better be a good kid because Mom and Dad are not getting along. I felt we were supposed to fix them." Many remember a general, all-pervasive feeling of anxiety that continues into adulthood.

Jennifer, a thirty-five-year-old mother of two, met me at a conference in the Midwest. I had requested an interview with her because her story seemed typical of many of those whose parents divorced when the children were young. We found each other in the crowd and moved to a corner of the conference room to talk. Jennifer fidgeted around in her chair. She seemed still childlike in her appearance and manner.

"Well," she said, getting right to the point, "I don't think my mom and dad's divorce was a big deal. Not the kind of nightmare some people have, you know. I know now that Dad was involved with someone else and Mom wasn't all that crazy about taking him back, so they divorced. I didn't think it affected me all that much—I was four when it happened—but now I'm really having trouble with my own kids and I feel it has something to do with the divorce."

I asked Jennifer to tell me more about her remembrances of her parents' divorce. She was the youngest of three, and at the time of the divorce, she felt that something terrible was happening and she did not understand it. It terrified her and didn't have a name. About this time, she began having nightmares and wetting the bed. She was never directly told that there were going to be changes, only that Daddy wouldn't live with them, but he would visit. "Despite all the reassurances, I felt as if the bottom of my stomach was falling out. To this day I can still remember that feeling. It seemed to last forever and affected me to the point that I had a lot of upset-stomach problems as a kid. The hard part was that both my folks kept telling me everything was going to be okay, but I didn't believe them because the ache in my stomach was louder."

Jennifer's ACOD issues began to surface after the birth of her last child. She found herself overwhelmed with anxiety every time she had to leave her children. For the first two years after her first child's birth, she left the child with someone else only three times. "My husband and I are in constant tension around my refusal to leave the kids. I know I should go out more, but every time I walk out the door I get that feeling in my stomach. I don't want to do to my kids what was done to me, but I can't enjoy myself when I am away from them, anyway."

Jennifer and I talk a little while longer. I am impressed with the fact that she knows intellectually that her anxious attachment to her children is probably not healthy for them. Yet she seems powerless to change her behavior until she goes back to deal with her family-of-origin issue. No amount of reassurance by her parents removed her sense of impending doom. Now it translates into a cling-clung relationship with her children. ACOD issues are indeed generational.

ACOD Issues

ACODs whose parents divorced in their preschool years say they mostly fear intimacy. They say they feel wary of making commitments and they carry fear inside them. Their fears are large and are about abandonment, humiliation, and rejection. Men still feel estranged from fathers. A major issue for them is lack of communication with their dads. As adults, they worry about giving adequate time to both parents. They feel anxiety that their marriages will be unstable because they are like their fathers. They struggle with low self-worth, resentment, and lack of assertiveness. Several ACODs feel they worked their whole lives to get the love and approval of a mother. They believe they are not worthy of love unless they work for it. In their marriages, they must give their "all" just to earn acceptance. Many, like Jennifer, smother their spouses and children with too much attention. They overcare.

These are some pretty huge abandonment issues for people who supposedly hardly knew the divorce was going on. I believe it proves that the divorce process extends beyond the actual separation of partners, and the effects of divorce continue beyond preschool for these ACODs.

Elementary School: Ages 6–13

Elementary school age children felt fear and confusion. They also felt relief. This theme appears in most of their stories. This age group felt oppressed in families where there was prolonged fighting. They were thankful that the bickering ended and sometimes furious for the circumstances and the behavior that finally accomplished the divorce. Children in this age group have a tendency to get on with life. Several ACODs remember being pragmatic. "I was upset for about a day, and then I knew it was the right thing for my folks to do." Said another, "I hoped everyone would use my parents' divorce as an excuse for my bad grades at school."

Confusion reigns in this age group's stories, and there is a pervasive sense of numbness. ACODs say their confusion was connected to wanting to be with a parent other than the custodial parent.

A thirty-year-old woman, Keri, whose parents divorced when she was seven, recalled the struggle she felt about spending time with her father. The divorce had been at her mother's instigation and she had custody of the daughter. "I felt so sorry for Dad. He seemed sad and lost. I thought by being with him I could make him happy," began her story. "One day I threw a huge temper tantrum in the backseat of the car. I cried and carried on that I wanted to live with Dad. Mom turned around from the front seat—by now, she had pulled off the highway and was stopped—looked me straight in the eye, and said, 'Your father and I have discussed this. We agree it is better for you to live with me. I have custody. You are going to live with me, not your father.'" Keri paused and took a deep breath. "You know," she continued, "I felt an enormous relief after my mom set her foot down. Somehow I didn't have to take care of my father. Someone older had set a limit, and I could let go."

I think Keri's story shows that part of the confusion for the elementary school child arises from the terror they feel when they think they have the power to make choices that should rightfully be adult choices. When Keri's mother set the limit, Keri went back to being a child and was relieved of the burden of compensating her father for his pain.

Other ACODs felt they were lied to about the divorce. It was frequently sprung on them. Several do not remember anyone's taking the time to explain what was happening. One was shipped off to a cousin's house, to be picked up two weeks later and taken to a home he had never seen. Those who were around constant fighting and physical abuse shut off all their feelings.

In some cases, mothers immediately began living with another man. The children remember confusion about the role of this man in their family. In some cases, new men provided relief and the assurance that financial needs would be met, a concern felt by a surprising number of these children. Many were scared of the future and angry because they did not receive the attention they needed.

ACOD Issues

Like the preschool child, intimacy looms in the stories from these ACODs when they describe their issues as adults. They say they have difficulty trusting and asking for help. As adults, they can be judgmental and black-and-white in their thinking. Men feel some animosity toward absent fathers, along with a fear they will be just like them. These adults are particular about who "family" is, tending to have difficulty accepting outsiders. Some feel uncomfortable in social situations, saying they lack the skills for small talk. They feel serious and "old" before their time. Many believe they grew up fast, became surrogate parents, and sacrificed their childhoods. Said one woman, "Here I am, thirty-eight years old, and I can be so competent and at the next minute so pathetic. I still feel ten." Several fear economic insecurity and wonder if they can make it on their own. They feel comfortable in the role of caretaker, even though they know the role is dysfunctional. A number of the women ACODs say they are just learning to have sexual relationships with their partners. They struggle with wanting a strong, passionate, sexual relationship, but fear getting lost in the other person or having the person leave. A great number of these ACODs say they don't know how to have a healthy relationship, and they worry that they will not know how to parent their own children effectively.

Adolescence: Ages 14–19

Teenagers appear to gravitate between anger and numbness. Those who were numb appear to be deeply affected by the dysfunction that had been going on for years before the actual divorce. In the words of a woman whose parents divorced when she was seventeen, "I was numb. By the time the divorce actually went through, I could no longer feel anything about it. I do remember the day it went through very clearly. I tried pot for the first time."

I spoke with this woman in a restaurant along with several other ACODs who agreed to meet with me and discuss their stories. Others clamored to add their piece. The theme of their discussion seemed to be "things I got away with during the divorce." One man added that he became sexually promiscuous during his parents' divorce process. This man, named Alex, seemed to speak for the others when he offered that he used sex to experience strong feelings and to escape his dysfunctional family's divorce. "It took my parents four years to actually separate—all through my high school years. By the time they actually did it, I was worn-out and completely disinterested. As far as I'm concerned, family life was put on hold that entire time."

Sherrie, another member of the group, spent her senior year of high school adjusting to three different sets of parents: her original parents, her mother and her mother's new husband, and her father and his new wife. In one year, she attended three different schools in three different states. "It was crazy and I was crazy, lost and doing drugs."

Those who felt anger admit that it was mixed with fear and some bravado. A woman who was fifteen says she was extremely angry, but of course she acted as if she weren't angry most of the time. She was also scared because her mother began drinking heavily and she felt abandoned by her father. Others were fearful that they would be expected to take care of their mothers, scared that their mothers could not make it alone. Some felt shame and embarrassment, but one young man thought he was "cool" because he came from a "broken home." There were special groups at his school for kids that lived with one parent, and he was "psyched" to join. He believes now that it was a kind of bravado he took on that masked the pain of the divorce for him. Some teens wrapped themselves up in an active social life. Others regressed, appearing younger than their age. Most teens endured the events leading up to the divorce for so many years they felt a mixture of relief and sadness at the actual event. Many say the divorce should have happened earlier.

ACOD Issues

As adults, the ACODs whose families divorced when they were teens feel "familyless." As a result, they work hard at ensuring the stability of their own marriages and families. Their feelings of deprivation are on several levels. They feel betrayed that the life they thought was "Ozzie and Harriet" was a lie. They feel no foundation for what they were taught. They feel appalled at whom their parents proved to be. Here is how one woman put it:

> I still feel ashamed, not so much about the divorce, as about my mom's craziness at the time, her radical change of behavior—she became irrationally assertive, like a kid going out on her own. I found all this terribly painful, the damage to her and her lack of self-esteem. My dad, in his male numbness and shame, seemed to be aloof from it all and relatively untouched, though sad. He didn't want any responsibility for his patronizing, bullying behavior, and he left crazies in his path.

Those ACODs who took mediator roles as teens tend to continue these roles in adulthood. They repeat a pattern that goes like this. They become close to people and involved in their troubles. They are usually welcomed because they know what they are talking about. The ACOD helps the people see all points of view and helps them fix whatever is causing their pain. The need for the ACOD is removed, the people leave, and the ACOD feels abandoned.

ACODs who were teenagers when their families split appear to have a more realistic view of the strengths and weaknesses of their parents. Many ACODs say they are actively developing and resolving relationships with both parents separately.

As with the other age groups, intimacy is a problem for these ACODs. They, too, feel fearful about getting too close to others. They risk intimacy only when they feel certain of someone, and they claim relationship addiction in high numbers.

They continue to search. They seek family, but they also seek something deeper. They look for roots. In the words of an ACOD whose parents divorced when he was twenty-two, "I have been searching for a path. I have not found a path that is for me. I have traveled from Tibet to Guatemala, New Zealand to China, looking for my inner truth, my path. Now I study medicine, wondering, what is the way? I am raveled and unraveled with many people along the way, looking for the root."

For some, the difficulty is simply where to stay when they go "home," whom will they spend what holidays with, mother or father? As ACODs get older, these choices seem more painful than they were earlier.

Finally, these ACODs have a fierce determination to make their marriages work. They fear divorce. Some ACODs have been divorced. On the whole, however, they say they work harder on their marriages. They feel a strong commitment not only to their spouses, but to their children as well. This group learned to desire family as a result of being children of divorce, and they seem to prize family in a special way.

Patterns of Age at Divorce

Does age at the time of the divorce result in any clearly identifiable patterns for the ACOD? The evidence is not conclusive, but I found some themes in the stories of these ACODs. First, depending upon their age, their issues seem to range from the more personal (for preschoolers) to the more global (for teenagers). With respect to parents, for example, ACODs who were between the ages of one and five when their parents divorced struggle as adults just to get to know the parent. ACODs who experienced the divorce when they were between six and thirteen feel angry and confused about their parents, while ACODs who were in their teens during the divorce believe they see their parents more clearly and realistically.

As for taking responsibility after the divorce, preschool ACODs feel abandonment, elementary school age ACODs feel like caretakers, and teen ACODs feel responsibility and fear. More elementary school ACODs fear economic insecurity than the other two groups.

Preschool ACODs still deal with fear of abandonment. The other two groups are fearful of relationships and understand that they have not had role models for healthy relationships.

All three groups dislike conflict, although teen ACODs step in to mediate sooner than the others. Preschool and elementary school ACODs are expert at anticipating conflict, and they tend actively to avoid it.

Overall, these three groups fear intimacy. They question their ability to form lasting relationships. They try to relate by caretaking, and they often experience abandonment. Some take the risk of asking for what they need in their relationships. Almost all have incredible insight into the effects the divorce has had on them. In this, they are hopeful. They believe they can live their lives differently. They work hard at taking the lessons from their past and applying them to the present.

Characteristics of Types of Divorce

I next want to look at the various styles of divorce because not all divorces are alike. This fact is obvious, even from the foregoing stories. As we examine the types of divorce, it is important to remember again that divorce is inherently neither bad nor good. We are focusing on the process, on the way in which the decision to separate was implemented. This process is a key factor in how the ACOD is affected and the extent to which he or she must confront issues generated by the divorce throughout life. For example, there is quite a difference between ACODs whose parents explained divorce and shared developments in the divorce process, and those whose parents shipped the children off to a relative and changed their entire domestic situation without the children's knowledge or participation. ACODs who were prepared feel more trusting of adults, whereas ACODs who had divorce sprung on them are more wary and on guard.

The dysfunction arising out of some divorce processes is generated in families. Issues not resolved in one generation carry over to other generations. We see this so clearly in the divorce process. Parents had a surprising variety of ways of separating. They did what made sense to them, sometimes with goodwill, sometimes operating out of gross dysfunction. As children, ACODs were the recipients of these behaviors.

For all ACODs, the ending of the family unit as they knew it is the core trauma. I have rarely seen a divorce that blunted this basic fact. The ending of the family *as the child knew it* always feels like loss, even when the family is severely dysfunctional. Nevertheless, there are more positive ways of making the painful transition away from what the ACOD knew as family to something else.

In this chapter we consider the most commonly described styles of divorce and their effects on the lives of ACODs. I think it is necessary to read the following stories without being judgmental. We have to marvel at the diversity of coping skills ACODs developed to adjust to their childhood experiences. Some of these skills proved dysfunctional in the long run, but enabled their survival at the time.

I have felt anger in reading some of these stories and I have learned compassion. More and more, my anger is turned outward to a society that has a part in the development and fostering of dysfunction in people. My compassion is for the real people of these stories who probably were doing their best with what they knew.

The Disappearing Parent

Elaine is forty-two years old. A strikingly tall woman with blond hair and green eyes, she has two children whom she raises alone since her husband's sudden death from cancer. Elaine feels she struggles with several ACOD issues. They began for her at age four.

When Elaine was four years old, her mother left overnight. Elaine asked the housekeeper, "Where has my mother gone?" The housekeeper responded, "I don't know." Elaine felt this response was the final word on the subject. Months later, Elaine's mother sent her letters saying that she loved her, but Elaine did not believe those letters because she reasoned that if her mother loved her, she would return home.

Elaine's father, a stern man, refused to discuss the disappearance of his wife. One day, several months after her mother left, Elaine's father announced, "Your mother and I have been divorced today," and he left the room. "When my father said the words 'your mother,' I felt slapped, as if *he* had never had anything to do with Mom, but it had something to do with me."

Elaine remembers that there was something unspoken in the house, that her mother had been a bad woman, and a poor mother. She sensed "women like her are terrible." Now she realizes that her mother was twenty-six years old when World War II ended. Elaine's mother was excited to be in touch with people, but her father returned from war a somber man. He became very fundamental in his religion. He believed life was to suffer, and his religion supported his belief. He wanted his wife to join him in his world view, but she could not. Where he was drab, she was dramatic and full of life. They were incompatible, and he eventually sent her away. Amazingly, she went without a fight, perhaps because divorce was not common in the 1950s.

While Elaine visited her mother, there was no contact at all between the two parents. Elaine's father would knock on the door and disappear, then her mother would open the door and take Elaine in. Elaine felt that door was a corridor in no-man's-land. Going to mother was going to another life. Her mother bought clothes for Elaine so she would not be embarrassed by the ragged outfits her father left her to wear. Her father was furious with the purchases. The first time Elaine's waist-length hair was cut, it was during a visit to her mother. Her father was again furious. He hurt Elaine by pulling and twisting her ear. She felt helpless to protect herself.

Elaine always felt fear around her father, even after she became an adult. She also felt abandoned by adults, for although grandparents and uncles knew what was happening, no one stepped in to help. They reasoned it was none of their business.

ACOD Issues

1. DON'T TRUST

Elaine believes she is still confronting trust problems as a result of her parents' divorce and her mother's disappearance. She says she is usually suspicious of people, fearing that they will not be honest with her. Also, she doesn't trust her own feelings. Elaine believes if she had let herself feel as a child, she would have gone crazy.

2. INSECURITY

In Elaine's story, there is constant insecurity around an abusive, custodial parent. She fears she is not worth knowing, and she expects her father to do to her what he did to her mother. Because his moods are unpredictable, she does not know how to act. Also, she never knows what will happen next. Although she fears her father, she is terrified that he will leave, too.

3. AS A WOMAN, TO ENJOY LIFE IS TO BE LIKE A WHORE

Elaine associates her joy and excitement, her feeling alive, with being wrong and dirty. Her mother's liveliness was punished. She is attracted to her mother's sense of life, yet she internalizes her father's disapproval. Elaine fears men.

4. TO STAND UP FOR ONESELF, IN RELATION TO ADULTS, IS DANGEROUS

Elaine felt at risk with her father. If she asserted her preferences, she was intimidated and physically hurt. Protective adults were nonexistent for her.

5. KEEP SECRETS/DON'T TALK/REPRESS FEELINGS

This repressive constellation may be the primary lesson Elaine received from her family. She learned that families perpetuate their dysfunction through silence. Then, by not feeling, the family lived as if they were normal. Nevertheless, it took enormous effort to keep down the feelings and maintain the secret. Elaine believes she has a lifetime of feelings to process, now that she is facing her ACOD issues.

6. AS A PARENT, BE PERFECT

Elaine determined that she would be the best mother in the world. She would never do anything to harm her children, and she would never leave them. She soon learned that her perfectionism was a burden for her, and for her children. After a while, they were seeking space from her, because they felt her hovering over them.

The Surprise Divorce

Ron is twenty-nine years old, athletically built, and a casual dresser. He seems at ease with himself, and a little shy at the same time. He is not married. He was engaged for two years and abruptly broke it off. He now devotes himself to his job, and to skiing in the winter and rock-climbing in the summer.

Ron's folks divorced when he was eighteen, the summer he graduated from high school. No one was more surprised than Ron. He assures me that he is not good material for a book on ACODs because, to this day, he does not understand what happened, really.

Ron says his story should be titled "We Were Happy Until . . ." His experience of his family is that they were close, open, and fun loving. His father worked in construction and later had his own company. Ron's mother stayed home to raise him and his brother. When the boys started high school, she took a job in a dentist's office. "We weren't wealthy, but we had enough money for some luxuries. We took family vacations several times a year. I have a good relationship with both my folks, and I've always felt I could talk with them." Ron thought they were a close family, and he felt secure in his family, but something went wrong in his senior year.

"The only way I can describe it is that my mother went wacko. She said she wanted her freedom, that she needed to search for her identity. She felt tied down with Dad." Apparently, to Ron, his mother underwent a metamorphosis that was entirely unexplainable. A woman who had appeared content was desperately unhappy and sought radical life changes. There was no dissuading her. She wanted out of her marriage. She filed for a divorce, and the entire process was completed within six months.

Ron is bewildered and angry. He was in shock at first. He struggles to understand this mother, whom he thought he knew, as she makes such a sudden shift. He wonders if he can trust his experience of his family. Is there some secret of which he was not aware? He is angry that his mother has done this to him, his father, and his brother. He believes that she has made them suffer unnecessarily. He is angry that she wants her own life. He doesn't know why it is so important to her to do these "crazy things" now. Why would she risk so much insecurity at her age?

Although the divorce happened when Ron was eighteen, he feels profoundly affected. He remembers that, immediately after the divorce, he retreated into a shell. He felt skittish around his friends, secretly wondering if people were going to pull away. He recently left a young woman to whom he had been engaged because he finds he has serious reservations about his ability to commit to marriage. Ron says his life feels in turmoil, and he doesn't believe he is ready for a long-term relationship. In the meantime, he maintains contact with both parents. He feels sorry for his dad, although recently Ron has seen his father in a new light, and he believes his mother had some legitimate grievances. He is still angry with his mother. He supports her search for more fulfillment, but he still blames her for his unhappiness. "She disrupted my ideal family. I have a hard time forgiving her for that."

ACOD Issues

1. What Is Real?

Ron and the ACODs who believed they had a happy family seriously question their perceptions after the surprise divorce. In some cases, parents who appear candid and loving to children are monsters to each other. Many ACODs bought into their parents' con and are devastated by the news of the divorce. They also wonder about their own gullibility. Why did they not pick up on what was happening? The divorce tests their ability to allow two true things to exist together: the children may have been happy, while one parent is miserable. In our self-centeredness, we believe that our experience has to be everyone's experience. This is not always the case.

2. WHOM CAN I TRUST?

Ron's trust in his family experience, and especially in his mother, is shaken to the core. He feels let down by his mother. He begins to erect walls around himself to protect himself from similar situations, and he becomes distant from friends. When he does trust, it is only after he has checked someone out, thoroughly. He is difficult to relate to at an intimate level because others sense from him that if they breach his trust, Ron will be devastated. In this he is controlling, and difficult to be around. Friends steer clear, not wanting to get into a trust bind with him.

3. WOMEN ARE UNDEPENDABLE AND FICKLE

Perhaps ACODs at large believe one parent or the other is undependable. In Ron's case, he feels less secure around women. He expects them to behave like his mother. He studies them for characteristics that could be interpreted as unstable. He generalizes to all women his experience with one, his mother.

4. RELATIONSHIPS CAN HURT

Ron has experienced pain from his parents' divorce. He recoils, withdraws for a time, then warily enters intimate relationships. Like many ACODs, the area of relationships is his greatest source of concern. Much of the divorce experience gets focused onto relationships and resolved there as well.

The Violent Divorce

According to recent studies, violence is on the increase in American families.[3] It takes all forms, verbal, physical, and psychological. John's family engaged in the entire range of violent behaviors. John is thirty-four, a social worker, and married, with two sons. He feels lucky to be alive, given his family background. He acknowledges that he has done hard personal work to be where he is today. All the odds were against him.

Violence was the cause of his parents' divorce. John's father, a successful attorney, began drinking heavily when the Securities Exchange Commission initiated an investigation that involved his law firm. The investigation extended over a three-year period, and John said he watched his father turn into a monster. "First he became silent and irritable. We walked on eggshells around him. As his drinking increased, his violence increased. He erupted into fits of temper, shouting at us at the dinner table, occasionally throwing a dish. My mother tried reasoning with him, but to no avail. Then both my parents argued, and Mom's drinking increased, also. The fighting and shouting lasted about a year. We lost a lot of dishware that year."

In the second and third year, the family's downward spiral progressed. John's father's business declined, perhaps because of the investigation, perhaps because of his alcoholism, or both. The house mortgage went unpaid for months. John's mother acted like a prisoner in the house, and all of them feared the wrath of John's father.

The verbal abuse gave way to physical abuse. Like many domestic-violence incidents, the first episode took place in the kitchen. John's father was already drunk. He insisted the meat loaf wasn't spicy enough. His wife replied that she'd made it the way she always did. "Don't tell me what I'm tasting, you bitch," said John's father, standing menacingly over his wife. He began slapping and hitting her. The children watched in terror. Then John and his sisters threw themselves at their father and between their struggling parents. John remembers, "Bodies were flailing everywhere. It is amazing that my father did as much damage as he did, with three of us piled on him." When it was over, both John and his mother were hospitalized. His mother had a skull fracture and broken ribs. John was beaten so badly that both his eyes were swollen shut, and his nose was broken. His father was in police custody.

This scenario was repeated several times in the next year. Everyone suffered. John's and his sisters' grades plummeted. They stopped inviting friends to the house after school, never knowing what to expect. John's mother grew depressed. She lost weight, and she paid less attention to her physical appearance. She filed for divorce, then became so depressed that it looked as if she would not carry it through. "Financial security was no longer an issue, as my father's business was going down the tubes," said John. "After he left, we kept the house, and then we sold it, because my mother could not make the payments. Our standard of living declined rapidly, but at least we were safe."

John's sisters moved away shortly after the divorce. John remained with his mother until he finished college. He worked his way through school and married soon after graduation. John worries about his marriage. He believes he wanted to prove he could do marriage better than his father, and he feared being alone. He married his wife barely three months after they met. They both admit it was infatuation. John and his wife fight, "but nothing physical, just shouting." Still, John worries about repeating his family's history.

ACOD Issues

1. BOUNDARIES ARE VAGUE

In the violent divorce, each person's personal space is invaded. Even when the fighting is only between the adults, the noise of it fills the house. It overflows into each child's room. John found he lost touch with the ability to set limits for himself, and his boundaries were not respected. Today, he has difficulty honoring his needs and asking for what he wants. When his wife seeks space and time alone, he feels it as a direct affront to him, instead of part of her healthy effort to take care of herself.

2. ANGER AND FIGHTING ARE NOT THE SAME

John's struggle, common to many ACODs, is how to handle his anger. He knows it is important to feel, yet his anger scares him. His only model, his father, lost control of his anger and became violent. John's anger is normal and may be an appropriate response to a situation in which he has been wronged. He can let himself feel his anger and express it in a place that is safe. Fighting may reduce the feelings, but it never resolves the basic issue. Fighting usually intensifies the basic issue and destroys safety.

3. CONFLICT IS FEARFUL. AVOID IT

In families that were permeated with violence, ACODs believed that differences of opinion and conflict could not be tolerated. Conflict is identified with violence and is, therefore, avoided at all costs. This belief can be very debilitating to ACODs in their relationships. Conflict is normal among people who are close and who care about each other. When ACODs repress conflict for fear of violence, their relationships become static and eventually lifeless.

4. INTIMACY IS FIGHTING

Frozen feelings are common in dysfunctional families. In the violent family, feelings erupt and are strong. ACODs know that fighting was the one connection their parents had, even though it was fearful. ACODs can grow up believing that one way to be close occurs through violence. Fighting can be seen as a test of intimacy and as a way of getting another's attention. In John's family, the one time they all pulled together as a unit was in fighting off John's father. He remembers such incidents as prime examples of closeness and cooperation. The danger is that as an adult, John will create similar scenes in order to have a feeling of intimacy.

The Late Divorce (We Stayed Together for the Sake of the Kids)

A number of ACODs in their twenties report that their parents divorced as soon as the children were old enough to be on their own. Linda's parents did exactly that. They waited until the last of their four children married, then they announced their divorce. They were fifty-seven years old, and they were worn-out from a relationship that had soured twenty years ago. They claimed they had only stayed together for the sake of the children.

So how did these children fare? According to Linda, not

so well. She says that it felt to her that she endured the divorce process throughout her entire childhood. She knew, intuitively, at an early age, that her parents were not happy together. They fought periodically. Her mother complained about "him" to relatives, amid much sighing and eye-rolling. As Linda grew older, her mother confided to her that if it had not been for the children, she would have left her husband long ago. Both partners suffered, and both had their ways of conveying it.

Linda's father spent his free time in his workshop. Linda's older sister functioned as a substitute wife to him, anticipating his needs, fixing him special meals, carrying dinner down to the workshop.

The tension in the house was pervasive. They were a family who lived in intimate isolation. "Talk about a crazy-maker!" said Linda. "We looked fine on the outside, especially to the neighbors. We even went through the rituals, birthday parties and graduations, but internally, we were so sick!"

As a teenager, Linda remembers asking her mother why she did not divorce her father. The answer, "Because of you kids," left Linda feeling more miserable and guilty. It was her fault her parents were so unhappy. She felt she was to blame. She suffered the same pain a three-year-old does who believes her parents divorce because the child isn't good enough. In Linda's case, those fears were confirmed. If she didn't exist, her parents would be happy. They would do what they wanted to do.

Linda feels punished by her parents' choice. They stayed together for her and her sisters, but the quality of life in the relationship was horrendous for the children. To Linda, it feels as if they were doing surgery with a dull kitchen knife, and the children suffered under this inept procedure. "I think I'd have been grateful if we'd had a wonderful life. The fact is, we were all miserable and worn down by their marriage. When I received word they were divorcing, I was truly relieved. I did feel some sadness, and it came as a shock after so many years together. I had become inured to their relationship."

Children whose parents stay together for their offspring are living with enemies. The parents are enemies to one another, and in reality, they are enemies of their children, as well. Children are stressed from living around threats, criticism, unspoken anger, and hatred. Side-taking is inevitable. Most children of divorce take sides at some time in the divorce process, but these children have the opportunity, and are often pressed, to take sides throughout their lives. Overall, their home environment is hostile territory, dominated by parents who have become enemies instead of collaborators. The psychological stress children experience in these settings is enormous. ACODs whose parents stayed together for the sake of the children appear emotionally shut down. This is understandable. They are like civilians in a war zone. They have lived in a climate of pervasive fear and uncertainty.

ACOD Issues

1. DENIAL

It has been interesting to learn that every ACOD I interviewed knew, at some point in their parents' divorce, exactly what was going on, then "forgot" it in order to fit in with the parents. The late-in-life divorce is a prime setup for learning about denial. Many ACODs felt they had to deny their perceptions in order to survive over such a long period of time. The problem then becomes that they learn denial as a way of operating in their adult life. Then ACODs ignore things they should pick up on in order to remain healthy in relationships.

2. LOVE MEANS SUFFERING IN SILENCE

Although Linda's mother was not silent about her unhappy marriage, many late divorcers are. ACODs can grow up believing there is something noble about hanging in with dysfunction. Long suffering and silence in the dysfunctional relationship only prolongs pain, which is very real for all involved. Unfortunately, divorcing people have not had much support in this area from religion. There seems to be a premium put on suffering, and it is praised. There is an apt phrase in addiction-recovery circles that goes, "In life, pain is inevitable. Suffering is a choice." The late-in-life divorcers refuse to accept the pain of their poor choice of a marriage partner. They punish themselves and their children by choosing to suffer. No one wins.

3. COMMITMENT MEANS INCARCERATION

Parents who stayed together for the sake of their children teach that commitments create prisons from which there is no release. Consequently, ACODs from these families are wary of commitment because they associate it with loss of freedom. They learn that their own commitment to their life process is not to be valued. It is little wonder that ACODs seek the perfect mate so they don't have to confront the ambiguity of constantly changing relationships.

4. IMPRESSION MANAGEMENT

Linda's family acted "as if" they were a family when they were in the public eye. ACODs can leave their families of origin and continue the process of presenting the image they think others want to see. Many ACODs became expert at pretending they were normal, while they were actually guessing at what normal might be. Linda said of her own marriage, "In many ways, I became a romance addict. I did things that looked good, with no regard for substance. My own marriage floundered, and my husband said he felt empty around me. He was right. I looked fine, but there was no one home for him to relate to."

5. LOWERED EXPECTATIONS

ACODs from late divorces experience a crisis in confidence with intimates. They fear they will not see people for who they are. Many feel betrayed by parents who feigned loyalty to one another. ACODs feel tricked. Consequently, they lower their expectations generally, and with regard to everyone they meet. They also become hypervigilant, constantly on guard lest they again be deceived. They experience a loss of trust and exhibit some cynicism about relationships. Inside, they feel sad that their trust in their parents was misplaced. It is hard for them to forgive these adults, and themselves.

Protect-the-Kids Divorce

I believe there may be a fifth type of divorce in which parents protect the kids by withholding information. This form is more subtle than the other four. In it, the parents agree that a mutual separation is best for themselves and the children. Then they withhold essential information from the children about the real reasons for the split. ACODs from these divorces are confused as adults. They resemble children who were sexually abused by an otherwise gentle, loving, upstanding parent. They have a hard time understanding why they feel so bad, because the divorce appeared to have been done "right."

These are "form as a fix" divorces. Parents believe that if they perform certain processes with their children, that in itself will insure a perfect outcome. During the divorce process, there are meetings with each parent separately with the children, then meetings with both parents. The form is right, but content is lacking. Techniques are used to give the impression that the family is communicating, but the truth is not being stated, so real communication is unlikely.

Monica's parents' divorce was of this type. After some mild tension and weeks of raised voices, Monica's parents met with her to tell her they were divorcing. Monica, thirteen, was shocked because she did not believe her parents were incompatible. Her parents communicated in the best style. They used "I statements." They were not accusatory. Each person had a chance to speak, and each was listened to respectfully. It boiled down to the fact that Monica's father was at a time in his life where he felt the need to explore, to be free, and to see the world. This puzzled Monica, as she thought he came and went rather freely already. Her parents did not seem to cling to one another, so why could he not be free and stay with them?

The divorce went through. Monica lived with her mother and saw her father periodically. When she was eighteen, she discovered that her father was gay. He had really left the marriage to explore his homosexuality. This information had not been shared directly with Monica. She was devastated by the news. "It was not the fact that he was gay that upset me, but the dishonesty that went on for years." Monica felt her parents did not trust her to understand and process information in her own way. Nor were they willing to relinquish control and let Monica see her father for who he really was.

The breach of trust was a major issue for Monica, as it is for many ACODs. Many ACODs were protected by parents who made unilateral decisions about how much information they could handle. In the long run, ACODs feel this process backfires and they are left with the psychological fallout. How much to tell is a touchy issue in divorce. At some ages, children would not even know how to process some kinds of information. Yet, for a thirteen-year-old, the leap from "Daddy wants to explore" to "Daddy is questioning his sexual orientation" is a pretty wide gap to bridge. In positive divorces, which I discuss in Chapter 9, ACODs describe parents who gave them accurate information that was appropriate to the age of the child. As the child grew older, more information was given along the way. Having a gay parent is only one of many sticky issues ACODs had to face as children. In those cases where parents answered children's questions as they arose and were honest, not controlling, ACODs feel secure in their relationship with their parents even when this information was painful. Except in families where there was out-and-out fighting, ACODs generally feel that they sensed more was going on between their parents than they were being told. This knowledge was true for children as young as three years.

The divorce process itself turns the child's world on end. Insecurity and anxiety, fear of the future, and fear of abandonment are common feelings for these children. Think how bewildering it is not to know the real reason for all the pain. No wonder ACODs feel confused.

A young woman who, throughout her life, received conflicting versions of her parents' divorce, finally resolved the issue in this way. She says, "I had to come to terms with my own view of what happened in the marriage that led to the divorce and not rely exclusively on my parents' version. This led me to allow myself a good marriage, while not expecting it to be a perfect one."

Dysfunction Permeates All Types

Not all divorces fit the five patterns of disappearing-parent, surprise, violent, late-in-life, or protect-the-kids divorce. These five are commonly heard, however. Some ACODs believe their parents did a combination of the five types. Each type is dysfunctional in that children and adults were harmed by processes that were secretive, controlling, abusive, and irresponsible. Inevitably, whenever divorcing parents became secretive and controlling with their children, the damage to trust was great.

The truth is sometimes painful. During divorce, some of the truths we have to face feel like failure. Still, ACODs have learned from experience that lying, covering up, and protecting have been very destructive to them. No truth ever hurt as much as the long-term erosion of their trust.

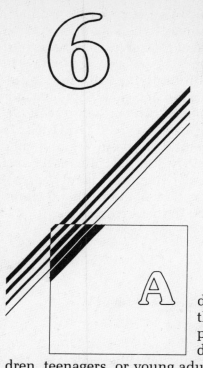

Adult Children of Divorce—The Characteristics

dult children of divorce—who are they? ACODs are adults whose parents divorced. They may have divorced when ACODs were children, teenagers, or young adults. As a result of the experience of divorce, they have developed a specific set of characteristics that affect their ability to form healthy relationships, marriages, and families of their own. In addition, ACODs carry these characteristics into their jobs and leisure time. ACODs are similar to adults whose childhoods were spent in addictive and dysfunctional families (ACOA) in that they developed certain attitudes and behaviors as children that helped them get through traumatic experiences. While these behaviors helped them survive their family's breakup when they were children, in adulthood they have become the very things that make their lives unmanageable and unhappy. For many ACODs, the only model they had for intimate relationships was their family of origin, whose patterns of relating before the divorce were often very destructive. Consequently, ACODs are likely to repeat those original patterns, often oblivious of how damaging they are to themselves and their loved ones.

ACODs share several characteristics. Some ACODs may exhibit a greater variety of these characteristics than others. Some "specialize" in just two or three. Others identify with all of them. These characteristics affect their lives now, as adults. Although ACODs developed them in response to a situation in childhood, they prevent ACODs from living fully in the present. Naming these characteristics is a first step in understanding why ACODs act and feel as they do. The presence of ACOD characteristics does not mean ACODs are "bad." ACODs may do harmful things to others when they unknowingly operate out of the characteristics, but they are not inherently bad people. They are sick from their dysfunctional family experience, and they are getting well as they confront the dysfunctional characteristics they took on in that experience.

The Characteristics

1. ACODs Have an Overdeveloped Sense of Responsibility

ACODs have become experts in taking responsibility. Unfortunately, they take responsibility for others far more frequently than they take responsibility for themselves. What was happening in childhood that so many ACODs became so overly responsible? When parents moved toward the decision to divorce, they had many needs that were overwhelming for them. They were preoccupied with their relationship and most of their attention was going to their own troubles. Consequently, the needs of parents overrode children's needs, at least during the three phases of the divorce.

Not only did parents have less time and attention for their children, they were often completely unavailable emotionally. Children soon found themselves wanting to be helpful, so they began to parent younger siblings and even their parents.

Josh, a young man whose parents divorced when he was sixteen, took a caretaker role readily. Even as he tells me about it, I feel his eagerness to be helpful. "I remember that I was really worried about my younger brother. I was also concerned about Mom. Could she make it on her own? Was she lonely? I

used to sit down with Mom and talk in a very adult fashion."
He laughs as he recalls this ritual of theirs. "I would make us
some refreshments and then I'd sit across from her and discuss
my brother—how was he doing in school, was he into drugs?
We had this conversation on a regular basis." I share with Josh
my question about what he felt he got out of their weekly tête-
à-tête. "Well," he drawls, "I remember I felt so helpless during
my folks' divorce. I just wanted to do something. I believed
Mom and Dad were helpless, too. I was shocked by this because I believed they should be strong. After all, they were the
adults, but they just weren't functioning that well. At least
worrying about my brother and being a friend to Mom were
things I could do. I guess I felt needed. That's what I got out of
it." "But what about you?" I ask. "Who took care of you?" Josh
seems surprised by my question. He waits a long time. Then he
answers, "I don't know. I never thought about it."

Another ACOD, a woman aged thirty-six, recalls that at
age four her parents divorced, and by age eight she was taking
care of one brother and two stepsisters. She washed dishes,
cooked, and spent weekends cleaning house and doing laundry. As she got older, she was not allowed to date because she
had to baby-sit her siblings. Nor was she allowed to do extra-
curricular activities at school, because they took time away
from chores. This woman married at age seventeen, not knowing much more than housework and caring for kids.

As ACODs parented their siblings and parents, they became little adults, serious and somber at home, acting the part
of the adult. Like Josh, they rarely asked themselves why they
took these roles, they just stepped into them. A woman who
found herself caring for four brothers at age eleven said she
was controlling and bossy about it and usually felt resentful
about having to care for them, but she believed her parents
were helpless, so she did it anyway.

Many ACODs' developmental needs were put on hold.
Thus, as adults, they react to things with the maturity of a ten-
year-old. ACODs had to grow up quickly and take responsibility before they were ready. Several young men who remained with their mothers report that they were told they were
the "man" of the house. They believed they should take their
father's place, yet they were scared. They did not know what to

do, but their mother's affirmation and dependency seemed to give them a place in the fragmented family.

In the divorcing family, children lose their playfulness. If the families were dysfunctional through the divorce process, the events of the divorce were not fun. It was a time of seriousness. Some ACODs escaped into a world of fantasy and imagination to return to playfulness. Others lived with a parent who didn't know how to support playing or who could not parent adequately. When children were playful, they were "out of control" and were hushed. As adults, it is difficult for ACODs to let loose of their inhibitions and completely let go. They experience pangs of guilt if they are having too much fun. Some ACODs played, in the face of disapproval, and took on the constant feeling that they were wrong or "bad."

For many ACODs the heavy sense of responsibility extended to the divorce itself. They had the illusion that the trouble was their fault. They thought they could repair the marriage if only they tried hard enough, if only they were good enough. Some believed they could make the fighting and tension stop by their behavior. They even believed they were the cause of the divorce. Some ACODs became invisible, believing in this way they could prevent the divorce. I have pondered this tendency of ACODs to assume responsibility for their parents' divorce, for it is a prevalent theme in their stories. Some tell me that the notion of their families' breaking up was so inconceivable that they searched themselves for the cause. Others remember that they attempted to absolve their parents of all responsibility, not wanting to see their parents as people who had needs. In protecting their parents, the children made themselves the cause. It alleviated some of the helplessness they were feeling. We have to marvel at the exalted image children must have of their own power. The belief that they were responsible for their parents' divorce led them to feel guilt and shame and to take responsibility for events, even when they did not cause them.

All this focusing on the needs of others results in ACODs' not developing a sense of themselves. It is a setup for codependency. ACODs spend more time externally focused than internally aware. They can reach their twenties and not realize they are separate human beings with their own identities.

As adults, ACODs carry heavy burdens, brought on by years of taking responsibility. Kristin, a thirty-six-year-old ACOD whose parents divorced when she was twelve, had made several appointments to speak with me and canceled each at the last minute. When she finally breezed into my office, on time, her first words were, "I'm sorry." My first words were, "I'm Diane." We both laughed. I was glad I had pursued this appointment with Kristin. I felt sure I was going to enjoy her and learn from her experience.

After collapsing into a chair, Kristin sighed and said, "I always do that. I'm always apologizing even before I know if I need to." She went on to tell me about her life. Her parents had divorced in the 1960s, and Kristin's mother had been ill prepared for both the divorce and for life after divorce. Kristin says at the time she believed she was to blame for both her mother's helplessness and the divorce. "I know it sounds crazy, but that is exactly how I feel. I have gone through life completely pressed down, carrying my mother's shame, because I caused my folks' divorce. The one thing my mother did for me during that period only made me feel worse. She put me in a Catholic school because she thought I'd get more attention. But in those days, divorce was still frowned upon by the administrators and teachers, who were mostly nuns, so not only did I feel guilty for the divorce, but I got hit with the Catholic shame trip. Needless to say, my self-esteem hit bottom in that situation."

I asked Kristin to tell me more about her sense that she caused her parents' divorce. Kristin played with the fringe on a lovely silk scarf that adorned her dress. She seemed lost in herself, thinking. When she spoke, it was with a directness that was disarming.

"If I had been 'enough,' my parents would have 'loved me enough' to work for my happiness. They didn't, and I feel like shit." She adds as an afterthought, "Now as an adult I will do anything to help others feel good. When they are miserable, I get even less from them."

Kristin told me she was troubled because she found herself saying "I'm sorry" for everything. This phrase has become a mantra for her. She uses it when she makes mistakes, when others make mistakes, or when she does not know what else to say. She takes responsibility for things that are not her responsibility, and she is always apologetic.

In response, I asked her about the link of overresponsibility and shame. Of course, when Kristin takes on others' lives, she takes on an impossible task, so she is constantly facing failure. She can't control their lives, nor their decisions. No wonder she feels as if she is not "enough."

Kristin had to cut one appointment short because she was late for another meeting. She told me she is always in a rush, overscheduling (again, she can never do enough). Before she left, she said, "You know, Diane, I've thought a lot about 'I'm sorry.' I always believed I was sorry to others for the messes in their lives. Today, I had a flash while we were speaking. I think I'm really saying 'I'm sorry' to myself. I'm sorry for beating up on myself for not doing something I couldn't do anyway."

Like Kristin, ACODs feel responsible for others' mistakes and try to make up for these mistakes, even though they are not theirs. Sometimes ACODs are not very direct. They escape relationships with others and with themselves by avoiding, withdrawing, and feeling guilty. So ACODs handle feelings by going away rather than confronting. A man whose parents divorced when he was six did not know the reason for the divorce until he was eighteen. Neither parent expressed anger at the other, nor did they discuss their relationship with the son. For years, the son agonized over what he could do to make up for their mistake. Finally, at eighteen, he acknowledged that his efforts had been futile and he had lived a life of guilt and shame. In a casual conversation, his father said, "Your mother and I knew we had made a mistake marrying two years after the wedding. We came from different worlds. Divorcing was the best thing we ever did." The young man was flabbergasted. He had spent twelve years in the agony of taking responsibility for something that was not his responsibility at all.

As children, ACODs are too young to take on others' pain. Children have enough to do just caring for themselves, and even in that, they need the help of adults. Many ACODs were frustrated in meeting their basic needs. When they took on responsibility for the adults, carried their burdens, and tried to control their lives, ACODs thwarted their own development in dramatic ways. Some acted out their pain maliciously. They inflicted pain on younger siblings, friends they cared deeply about, even helpless animals. It takes a long time to forgive oneself for such activities, but it is essential to do so.

ACODs do not discriminate properly when it comes to taking responsibility. They are greedy. They take it all. Ultimately, this characteristic does not get them what they think they want. Their attempts at responsibility are really attempts at control. The relationships ACODs thought they could preserve eluded them as children, even as they elude them as adults. ACODs live rigidly because they are always on the lookout for others and their needs. Gradually, as ACODs recover from the ACOD past, they learn how to take responsibility for themselves and to unhook from taking care of others. In doing so, there will be some pain as they see the loss of their childhood and their playfulness, and they will also be able to experience joy. For some, it will be for the first time.

2. ACODs Attempt to Control Everything

Control is closely linked with taking responsibility. In fact, attempting to control everything and taking excessive responsibility are the two key characteristics of ACODs. They are like the two poles holding up a tennis net. All the other characteristics float between them. They hold the ACOD profile in place.

Control was frequently an issue in divorcing families. To the extent that families were dysfunctional, they felt chaotic. Some ACODs lived in families where there was no order and there were no limits. Others were in rigidly controlled settings. Both situations left children with huge control needs. No matter how hard children tried, nothing they did prevented their parents' divorce. This realization did not thwart their attempts at control, it only made them stronger.

When I think about divorcing families and control, I remember Andre, a man in his early forties. He gave me a new appreciation for the effect of chaos in the divorcing family and the resulting attempts at control on the part of ACODs. Andre was the oldest of three boys. His family lived in a midwestern city, in the suburbs. Both parents worked. His father was an executive in a manufacturing company, his mother a supervisor of a clerical pool for a large corporation. "Because both of my parents worked, we had a kind of order to our family. We ate the evening meals at regular times, we all had chores we did. My brothers and I played sports and Dad drove us to practice. We had to do homework and TV was rationed. You couldn't watch it until your homework was done. I guess we were just your normal everyday family."

This picture changed dramatically during the predivorce period. Andre recalls waking up one day to a changed family. His parents had been keeping a lot from their children, aged twelve, nine, and seven. To their children, their relationship seemed normal. Underneath, they were struggling. Andre's father had been involved in several affairs. He now wanted out of the marriage. Andre awakened to his father's shouting and his mother's crying. The sounds traveled the length of the house as his mother followed his father from room to room. Doors were slamming behind them. "I lay in my bed, just terrified by what I was hearing. Their fighting really scared me. I wanted to crawl under the sheets and never come out." Soon Andre's mother came into the bedroom. She was crying and she told her sons that their father was leaving for a while. He was moving across town. She did not know if he would come back.

After this event, which began a two-year predivorce period, the family's life was totally unpredictable. I press Andre to give me some specifics. "Our structure as a family went down the tubes. Meals were never regular because Mom worked another job three nights a week. We lived on fast food. I never knew if we would get to soccer practice. Sometimes she'd say she could take us, sometimes Dad said he'd come by. Then they would get their signals crossed and no one would come, or I'd think they weren't coming and call a friend, and at the last minute, Dad would arrive. Then Mom began to lose it, I think. Our house was a mess. We all stopped doing our chores. I didn't have the energy to do my laundry and I wore dirty clothes for weeks at a time. The pile of dirty clothes got so large I couldn't face it until I was desperate for clean clothes. I feel like we were in shock and just walking around like zombies. At least I felt that way. I didn't feel any energy and Dad was gone most of the time and Mom was, too, at work. It was like we were barely functioning and we were confused inside and out."

The chaos of the household mirrored the inner turmoil of the family members. Andre's story is typical of many ACODs' in that the divorce process changes the pattern of relationships along with usual family patterns. Andre is different from many ACODs who exerted greater attempts at control, believing that they could save the family. He became listless and depressed. He felt overwhelmed by the confusion. Andre became increasingly disengaged from school. His grades suffered and he withdrew from sports, his one love. By the time he appeared at our scheduled interview, his childhood issues had become ones of excessive control in adulthood.

"If you want to know what I really want, I really want to find a relationship that I can count on and that will stay the same. If I could find and preserve the perfect woman in a moment in time, I would do so. When I think of change, I remember the chaos of my family. I never want to do that to anyone, and I don't want it done to me. I just want control!"

Andre is grinning at me as he says this, but I feel he is deadly serious. He wants to counteract the upheaval of his childhood divorce experience with absolute predictability as an adult. These sentiments are heard among scores of ACODs.

The area of relationships is a key area for control. In the wish not to repeat parents' mistakes, ACODs believe there is something they can do that will make people stay with them, or act acceptably or be happy. One ACOD wrote that she wanted to freeze-frame her relationship with her mother. She was afraid that any major change would burst her bubble. This woman was a recovering alcoholic and had recently come out as lesbian. She decided that her mother could not handle knowing who her daughter really was, and this ACOD was not willing to risk abandonment by her mother. Then she would have no family at all. Consequently, she carefully controlled the information she gave her mother. In the process, their intimacy declined and they related superficially. In the end, the ACOD kept control of the relationship and lost the closeness and "family" feeling she believed she was preserving.

One ACOD worries that things will happen to her children and her husband when she is not with them. She actually wants to be able to control nature, runaway vehicles, and household accidents. She says she has a tendency to worry over things she has no control over, letting them control her. As a result, she has periods of anxiety and sleepless nights.

Another ACOD has trouble accepting outsiders as family. His father is an open and generous man who tends to include people from the "highways and byways" in family affairs. This young man has decided what a family is and his father is not cooperating, he is not under the ACOD's control. To cope with this, the young man ignores the outsiders and pretends they aren't there.

When ACODs are immersed in their illusion of control, they believe there is something they can do to make things right. This is understandable, for they went to extremes in their dysfunctional families to make things right. Usually, they were frustrated in those efforts. A small-business owner confided that he bumped up against his ACOD control issues on a daily basis. He believes his way is better. His attitude is: "My way or no way." Supporting this trait is extreme perfectionism. His control and his perfectionism are a deadly combination in a businessman. Needless to say, he has a constant turnover of employees because no one ever meets his standards. Nor can they read his mind enough to suit him. This behavior has almost brought his business into bankruptcy, and it is a source of continual pain and frustration for him.

A young woman who was shuttled between foster homes as a child believed she would win back her original parents if she "did it right" in school. She thought her parents would be so proud of her they would take her into one of their homes. She set out to get A's, got elected to the student council, and was a National Honor Society member. Although these achievements did bring her some glory, they did not bring back her parents, for her mother had formed a new family and her father had disappeared.

Some ACODs react to their childhood experiences of divorce and its resulting confusion by moving into rigidity. They mistakenly believe that the antidote for chaos is control. Many ACODs relate the fact that they seek groups known for their rigidity with the hope that they can achieve some order in their lives. Thirty-year-old Jack, whose parents divorced when he was seven, has chosen a highly rigid and controlling life-style in Orthodox Judaism. Other ACODs say they joined the military looking for structure and an end to the confusion of their families.

Some ACODs practice their controlling on other people as well. Side by side with his rigid lifestyle in Orthodox Judaism, Jack maintains a marriage to an active addict. He is trying to control her behavior with religion. ACODs seek relationships with needy people and then spend years trying to help them. A twenty-four-year-old ACOD pondered this pattern in his life. He said that he felt so helpless in his efforts to "fix" his parents that he transferred his helping to all his other relationships. He said he had an uncanny knack for picking out needy people even when they looked good on the outside.

It is important to see the common element in all the above examples of controlling: ACODs control in order not to feel their own feelings. Their efforts to control keep them busy with the illusion that they can make a difference. But the evidence of all ACOD stories is just the opposite. The more they control, the less they get what they want. Their adult relationships and situations frustrate them as much as did their family of origin. Ultimately, they are thrown back on themselves and their own pain. Focusing outside themselves on others only keeps them away from doing their essential inner work, a work only they can do.

3. ACODs Fear Conflict

The nature of divorce is that two people have incompati-ble needs that cannot be satisfied in their marriage. Conse-quently, conflict is basic to the divorce process. Conflict does not have to be carried out in a manner that is destructive or fearful. Nevertheless, most ACODs experienced the dysfunc-tional aspects of conflict. Because conflict was often accom-panied by anger and violence, its lessons are strongly im-printed on ACODs' memories. At the very least, parents who were continually fighting left ACODs with the impression that fighting was a way to solve conflict. It was a powerful model, even if it did not work.

In most divorcing families, conflict was not safe. It became violent, vicious, scary. ACODs witnessed physical and/or verbal violence. Sometimes children were hurt physically or watched a parent being hurt. For ACODs, conflict had no bounds and was unpredictable. It seemed to rise up when children were least expecting it. Consequently, they became exceptionally observant, looking for signs and clues about a fight brewing.

Liza, who was fourteen when her parents finalized their divorce, says she can still recall her physical terror over her parents' shouting and threats. "I come from a family where anger was okay. We weren't told to keep our anger down, but in the later stages of Mom and Dad's divorce they both got verbally vicious with each other. There was a streak of meanness in them I had never seen before. I was scared to death to be around it. In the beginning, I would hide in my room, but I could still hear them fighting, and sometimes they would drag me into it by wanting me to vouch for one of them. Then I got to the point that if I knew Mom was coming over (Liza lived with her father during the predivorce separation phase), I got out of the house and stayed with a friend."

The trauma around Liza's parents' conflict resulted in Liza's developing two skills that she began using with other adults. She developed built-in radar that was constantly tuned into the slightest variations of mood on the part of adults. She could tell, for example, whether her high school teachers were annoyed, tired, or happy. Her second skill was as a people pleaser, which she used to avoid anger directed at her.

An ACOD who lived with her mother after the divorce got the brunt of the mother's unresolved anger throughout the postdivorce phase. She remembers that she would arrive home from elementary school, greet her mother in the living room, and pass into her bedroom to change into play clothes. Before she could get back out the door, her mother was raging at her for reasons that were incomprehensible. As a child, this ACOD became an astute observer of the smallest changes in her mother's demeanor, in order to flee before being subjected to the mother's anger. She never understood her mother's rage. Although it was directed at the child, it was never caused by the child. Nevertheless, this ACOD felt she was to blame, and she grew up attempting to mitigate the "storm factors" before they hit. She became externally referenced to the extreme, picking up on others' moods long before they were aware of their own feelings. An intense fear of conflict had molded this child into an excessively vigilant adult.

Conflict is so terrifying for ACODs because their parents, unto whom children have entrusted their safety, lost control of their anger. They could not take care of, or protect, themselves. How could they do the same for their children? And as the example above shows, parents do not always restrict their angry feelings to their spouse. If divorcing parents took appropriate responsibility for themselves, there would be less dumping of feelings on children, but that is not always the case. Consequently, children pick up many feelings they do not cause.

In some families, the conflict during divorce was not overt. Just the same, anger pervaded everything. One ACOD described her father as a "rageaholic." He met the world with one response—rage. She says she feared his rage and also knew, deep inside, that his rage had nothing to do with her (he was under great stress with the divorce), even though it was frequently directed at her.

In many divorces, especially those where parents tried to protect their children or "do divorce right," conflict was hidden and anger was suppressed. Several ACODs were in situations where both parents denied their anger, yet it came out sideways all the time. Ezra, a gawky young man of twenty-four, says he came from such a family. His parents divorced when he was sixteen. He is thoughtful in describing his situation. "Surely my family is one of those where dysfunction caused the divorce," he observed. "When it came to anger, we kids were taught that it just wasn't appropriate to raise your voice or lose your temper. If we did, my mother would say, 'We'll have none of that here, young man.' Anyway, both my folks kept everything in. I really believe their divorce was just the result of hundreds of little things they wouldn't say to each other—lots of little angers is the way I think about it."

Ezra was taught that anger wasn't allowed, but he experienced his parents as constantly "pissed." He says, "The worst thing for me is that I felt crazy because my perceptions were denied. I walked on eggshells around my folks."

ACODs who say they rarely saw angry behavior, yet felt it subtly present during all phases of the divorce, are fearful around anger and the prospect of anger. This has proved very confusing for them, and like Ezra, who "walked on eggshells," they feel crazy about trusting their perceptions. Some ACODs are more anxious about conflict when it is hidden than if it is expressed in outright fighting. Where anger was suppressed, there were vague messages and clues to be picked up. Some find it takes years to decipher the "code," and they understand the messages only in adulthood.

A thirty-eight-year-old ACOD reflects this issue in her story. She says that conflict was nonexistent between her parents, and fighting was not allowed. She never heard a raised voice in eighteen years in her household. Anger, on the other hand, was everywhere. "We were all like time bombs, just waiting to go off, and we knew that about one another." Another ACOD says in his family there was no conflict because there was no communication. His parents stopped talking two years before the divorce and rarely communicated afterward. Still, what he remembers is their tone of voice, their facial gestures, the hard-set line of his father's mouth. He knew his father was smoldering inside. This ACOD never experienced a moment of physical violence in his family, yet he cowers whenever anyone shows the slightest annoyance with him, or with someone else. He expects the worst.

"Part of not trusting my own perceptions about anger came from a family rule," claims a woman whose parents divorced after years of fighting. "We were always told we could not talk back. This meant that we had to accept our parents' view of the situation even when it differed from our own. In my family, the undercurrent of anger was always there, but the truth of it was hidden."

In some divorcing families, children learned to use conflict to perpetuate their dysfunction. A twenty-year-old ACOD, wise beyond her years, observed that conflict and crises usually kept her family occupied. They were so busy fighting and making up from the fight that they neglected to deal with the deeper issues they needed to address as a family. "It helped us externalize the problem and put it 'out there,' instead of taking responsibility for ourselves individually. Also, the blaming—

you caused it; no, *you* caused it—kept my parents locked into dysfunction for years."

Another ACOD says she learned to use conflict as a way to get her mother angry because, in so doing, she finally got some attention from her mother. "I felt I had no other way of getting her to see I existed. I would push her until she erupted. At least then she was focusing on me and not so much on the divorce." All of these issues affect ACODs as adults. Many of them have difficulty just expressing displeasure, much less anger. Standing up for their rights is even farther beyond their reach. Says one ACOD, "I respond with tears first and become a little wimp." Another ACOD says that she gets tense when there is any hint of conflict, and she does anything to avoid it. She often finds herself in the role of mediator, a role she played in her family. She tries to smooth over the conflict and help the two parties come to agreement.

An ACOD man whose parents' divorce was sprung on him at the last minute has a different reaction. He says, "I always blow every conflict out of proportion. A simple argument with my wife automatically means divorce. Last week we disagreed on some small issue. I left for work in a huff. By the time I got home later that evening, I had the divorce papers drawn up in my mind." Imagine his surprise when his wife met him at the door and calmly announced she had been thinking about their fight and felt she needed to apologize to him for her lack of responsibility around the issue! "She didn't see the argument as the end of our relationship. In fact, she thought it was helpful in clarifying some issues we had." This man was astounded at how readily he projected his ACOD past on his present relationship, and how quickly he was prepared to act it out.

Occasionally, ACODs learned to use conflict as a way to gain access to their feelings. Those who grew up in emotionally numb homes seek and even invite conflict as a way to feel alive and to feel they are interacting.

Len, an ACOD who volunteered his story to me, is a good example of this paradigm. He says that the one thing that remained constant throughout all the phases of his parents' divorce was fighting. "They fought even after the divorce was finalized and they didn't need to fight. I really believe that the only connection they had with each other was conflict. Their relationship was dead and had been for years." Len relates that after a time, he noticed a pattern in his parents' fights. There was the working up to the fight, during which they complained to the children about what the other spouse had done. Then there was the actual fight, which usually entailed shouting, some pushing, and threats. Then one parent would go away. Finally, after a few days, the instigator would initiate an apology and there was the making up. "My folks were always at some point on this conflict continuum," Len remembered.

In relationships, ACODs tend to confuse fighting with intimacy. Some believe that if you care, you fight, and some relationships feel dead except when there is fighting. Fighting erupts in high emotion. There is a flood of feeling and words rarely said. There is the climax of the fight and then the tenderness of making up. In ACOD families, this pattern may have been the only connecting the children witnessed. Then, ACODs tend to carry the same pattern into their relationships, believing they are close when they fight. For example, it is not unusual for children who were punished or even battered to seek battering and punishment because it was the only source of contact with their parents, and any contact, no matter how destructive, is better than no contact. Fighting serves the same purpose for some ACODs.

Conflict, fighting, and anger are found in healthy relationships. However, when they are the sole means of intimacy, ACODs need to look at the role conflict has in blocking their process of taking responsibility for their feelings and their lives. Conflict is a huge issue for almost every ACOD. Whether it was overt or hidden, whether erupting everywhere or coming out in subtle ways, conflict was rarely done in a healthy, productive manner. No wonder ACODs both fear it and use it. Facing the feelings and the issues around conflict is one of the key issues ACODs need to resolve in their recovery process.

4. ACODs Take Sides

As their parents were divorcing, ACODs felt torn apart. Sometimes children blamed one or the other parent, trying to make sense out of the pain they were feeling. They thought it might help the "wronged" parent to feel supported. Other children purposely tried not to take sides. They determined to be fair. In so doing, they may deliberately have blinded themselves to seeing what was really going on in their families.

One of the ways ACODs became hooked into their parents' conflict was through carrying information for them. Many ACODs recall shuttling between their parents with messages intended for the ex-spouse. Relates one ACOD, "Sometimes they were messages as simple as the dates for the school play, but increasingly they were important things like 'Why haven't I received the child support check?'" Another suggests, "I believe my mother thought she had more leverage if she conveyed her needs through me because my father adored me and hated her."

For ACODs, the messenger role is a trap. It feels as if it is helpful, yet it puts the child in the untenable position of operating as the go-between. The child does the communication tasks that belong to the parents and should be done by them. One woman believes her skill at carrying information between her parents led to her becoming a stage manager at a regional theater. There, she was able to make a living doing the very thing she had done as a child! However, she soon discovered that carrying messages between groups was exhausting. She could never do it satisfactorily because her messenger service prevented the people who needed to speak face-to-face from getting together.

Sometimes ACODs formed coalitions with one parent or with siblings. They might have done this to get even with the parent they perceived was hurtful. Children became confidants, especially when one parent was hurting. Again, children grew up fast, lending an ear to a parent who poured out troubles to them or who subtly presented information in such a way that children felt the parent was a victim. An ACOD who had carried information for fifteen years between her parents said, "My father did not hook me into collaborating with him against my mother. I did it freely. I was so eager to belong somewhere, with someone, and he offered me that possibility. I leapt at it." Another ACOD feels she joined with her mother against her father because she felt sorry for her mother and she felt she could promote peace and reduce conflict by "outnumbering" her father.

A more covert way of taking sides is spying, and some

ACODs did this as well. ACODs spied when they carried secret information of which one parent was not aware. Amy told me about her experience as a spy when we met in a park. Amy, whose parents divorced when she was thirteen, is twenty-nine. A stockbroker in a well-known firm, she is enthusiastic about this, her first, job. She pushed long auburn hair back off her face and began to tell me about her parents' divorce. "The first thing I want to say," she began, "is that it's pretty painful to go back over this stuff from my childhood. I had a lot of pain I had to work through, and I don't like to even remember it, if I can avoid it." I thanked Amy for her willingness to speak with me, and I suggested that maybe it no longer fits for her to share her experiences. Should we just have lunch and forget the interview? She paused, thought a moment, then said, "No, I want to do this. It's okay." I proceeded gingerly by asking her to tell me about those aspects of her childhood she feels comfortable discussing.

"If you want to know about spies and secrets, I'm your girl," she said, shaking her head with conviction. "I came from a long line of secret-keepers, and I guess I was a double agent," she said with a laugh. "Prior to my parents' divorce, I participated in subterfuge, secrecy, and cover-up for my father for his extramarital affairs. I was, in a sense, "primed" for this, as I am also an incest survivor." (Amy was five when the incest began.) "As an incest victim, I was told by my father that his sexual molestation was our secret and should not be shared with anyone. So it didn't seem so bad to keep the secret about his affairs when I was twelve. It was just another one of our secrets."

Amy's parents' divorce was hotly contested and dragged on because it took place in a state that does not have a no-fault system. Therefore, both custody and financial arrangements rode on one party's showing the other party as unfit. It was late in the predivorce period that Amy shifted her allegiance from her father to her mother. "I'm really not sure why I stopped covering for him. I did feel sorry for Mom, and I think I was so angry that he was willing to risk my happiness for a new woman." At this point, the divorce proceedings were going full swing, and now Amy regularly carried information to her mother about her father's activities. "And here's the crazy thing," Amy said. "My mother talked to me the same way as my father. She said that what I told her was 'our secret' and not to tell Dad I was doing it." After the divorce, Amy continued to share details of her father's life with her mother. "We were really tight, Mom and me, but as I got to college age, I felt I needed some space of my own. Mom said we were soul mates and understood each other." Amy looked troubled as she said this. "I guess it was good, having a mom to be close to, but sometimes I felt smothered and like I needed to get away from her and from my dad. Worst of all, for years I wondered about two things. One was would they have gotten a divorce if I hadn't carried Dad's secrets to Mom? And two, did Mom love me for who I was or because I did what she wanted? I still don't know."

Many ACODs felt powerless as their parents were divorcing. Spying, carrying information, and forming coalitions taught them that information is power. They learned to manipulate people with what they knew and became adept at pumping people for information. Then they used the information, occasionally to get revenge. Some ACODs remember using what someone else told them to hurt others. This is a pattern first learned in their families and continued in subsequent relationships.

Some ACODs were thoroughly confused by side-taking. Like Amy, they felt pressure from one or both parents to line up with them, yet neither side felt safe. An ACOD says he remembers taking sides against whomever he was angry with at the time. Another believes she was getting so many mixed messages she had to seek the truth on her own. Still, after she got the truth, she would then quickly take a side. Another ACOD says she did not know what the sides were, she just gravitated to her mother for emotional comfort.

As adults, ACODs face many tricky issues around the topic of sides. Most ACODs have a strong desire to belong. In daily life, at work and in relationships, they may find themselves drawn into conflicts or taking sides on issues that may actually be irrelevant. An ACOD who is well on the road to recovery confided that he found himself taking sides at work until one day he asked himself if he really cared about the issues on the two sides. The answer was a resounding no. He had just joined a side because he could not stand to be alone. That felt intolerable to him. He decided to stay with his realization, and he soon found, to his surprise, that there were usually more than two sides. There were multiple options involved in most issues. In several cases, he simply did not care. As he confronted his fears, left over from his experience of his parents' divorce, he had less internal pressure to belong somewhere.

The other issue ACODs face is that their very skills in communication, which may keep them in others' good graces, are ultimately harmful even to those they serve. No doubt ACODs receive praise and support for mediating, being go-betweens, and carrying information. But in this behavior, others are prevented from taking responsibility for themselves. Consequently, the ACODs "helpful behavior" props up others' dysfunctional behavior. In the long run, ACODs harm themselves, too, for they get their identity from a role, and not from inside. Taking sides is a poor substitute for the most basic "side"—my side. When ACODs are dedicated to taking responsibility for themselves, they find that they are much less enamored with belonging to groups or coalitions whose issues do not concern them. Part of the process of healing from the ACOD past is becoming clear about the issues that were solely the parents', and detaching from them. Although this detachment was difficult for ACODs as children, it is essential for them as adults.

5. ACODs Feel Abandoned

Abandonment is one of the largest issues ACODs face. It goes deep and wide. During their parents' divorce, there was less and less time for the children's needs as adult needs became preeminent. Children had the feeling that no one respected their needs. They felt abandoned physically and emotionally. Often, they were.

It is important to distinguish between change and abandonment. Divorce is a process that inevitably introduces change into the child's life. Change is not necessarily abandonment, even though when one is small and feeling insecure, any change can be threatening and feel like abandonment. Having said this, it is still true that ACODs were left by adults and felt dreadfully alone without their usual supports.

Physically, their usual caretakers disappeared. In many cases, fathers were gone and mothers had more responsibility for the family's livelihood. Whichever parent children lived with seemed less available due to the strain of their altered lifestyle. Sometimes, the child's actual lifestyle was disrupted in such a way that their physical needs went unmet. They had fewer new clothes, meals became erratic, they found themselves on their own.

Several ACODs write of their seeking nurturance from other mothers in the neighborhood. Some of these others that they looked to let them down or were dangerous. While some neighbors did provide support, some ACODs reported being sexually abused by men in their neighborhood whose homes seemed, at first, to provide a homey, safe atmosphere. Some ACODs went to grandparents, seeking stability and warmth, only to have a beloved grandparent die soon afterward.

Then there was the emotional abandonment. Often parents were so unhappy, their lives so stressful, that they simply detached from their feelings; they were not present emotionally. Consequently, they were unavailable to their children.

Sean is a young man who says his abandonment issues are huge. Like several ACODs whom I interviewed "on the run," he met me at an airport. I was eager to speak with him because he had sent me a detailed response to my questionnaire on ACOD issues. I had several hours between planes, so we found a deserted boarding area and settled in to talk. "I'm ready to go," he volunteered. "What do you want to know?" I told him I was interested in the issues that ACODs have to struggle with as adults, but suggested he start with his childhood, his parents' divorce, and his memories of that time. Sean said okay and launched forth. He told me he was an only child. His father was a physician, his mother a homemaker. The pre-divorce process took several years, culminating when Sean was sixteen.

"I was never abandoned in terms of physical things," said Sean. "In fact, the more our family came apart, the more stuff I got. I guess they wanted to give me something, but they couldn't think what, so it was material stuff. I had every technological toy ever made. I did get some good junk out of their divorce," he said, grinning. "But," he added, his voice cracking, "what I lost in my folks' divorce was my dad." I asked him to tell me more. "Because my dad was a doc, he wasn't home that much, so I never expected to see him that much. When he was home, he was a real pal, and what I liked best was that we'd always take a vacation together, just him and me, and those were great. We'd fish, we'd hike. Once, we canoed the Boundary Waters of Minnesota. It was the one time I knew he was there for me. I loved it and I loved our trips."

What followed in Sean's story is one of the inexplicable results of divorce. Sean was sixteen when his father initiated the divorce to marry a woman who was an acquaintance of the family. Sean was shocked by his father's decision. He didn't feel comfortable with the new woman in his father's life, and he felt betrayed by his father. "Dad didn't tell me about the divorce until it was almost a fact. I thought we were close, and it really hurt that he kept this from me for so long. But the most terrible part for me was that both my parents just shut down. They put on brave faces and tried to make the best of it. I really don't know if they had feelings about the whole thing or not." I observed to Sean that it sounded like his mom and dad shut down emotionally. Instead of feeling their emotions, they detached and became blank. "Yeah," he confirmed, "they were kinda like robots. When I saw how gone they were, I felt so scared. I had a lot of feelings about their divorce, but how could I tell them? It didn't seem like they could hear me, and I figured I just added to their pain. So I just went into myself. I was real moody. My girlfriend hated to be around me."

Sean lived with his mother and visited his father regularly, but after the divorce he felt he lost a vital connection. His father was busy with a second new family, and the yearly vacations with just the two of them ended. "This was really devastating for me. I was at a point in my life where I just longed for someone to talk to about life and growing up." Sean paused, then he said, "I miss my dad and the connection I thought we had. After the divorce, I had no orientation about my life. I felt that everything that went on outside got into my insides. There was nothing between me and the outside world. My parents were gone emotionally, especially my dad, and I never felt safe or protected from that time on. In fact, I still don't and I'm almost thirty."

Sean's story is one I heard over and over. Whether the abandonment was physical or emotional, or both, it resulted in children feeling terrified for their safety and without essential supports for their lives.

ACODs should not underestimate what it means that their most significant others left them. In the words of a fifty-two-year-old ACOD who still struggles with abandonment issues: "No matter how many people are around me, I still feel very alone." Many ACODs got the message that they were expendable. They believed they had little worth. They found themselves without essential supports, and those they were most vulnerable to were the least able to help them. In some cases, parents actively abused their children.

How do these childhood abandonment issues play out in adulthood? ACODs enter adult life still carrying the fear of abandonment. One ACOD put it this way: "I feel I am not worth loving. In my relationships I feel temporary. I believe my partner is just staying with me until something better comes along."

Many ACODs struggle with similar feelings. They live in constant fear that they will be left to handle things alone. This fear then manifests itself either in refusing to take responsibility for things, or becoming overly responsible and caretaking when such activity is inappropriate. An ACOD man shared a story that I heard repeatedly: "I have a tremendous need for approval from persons I feel close to. I am only able to love one person at a time. I latch on to the other person, then set myself up to be a victim, then in turn I victimize the other person. This, of course, results in the other person's leaving me, and I say, 'See, abandoned again!'"

Abandonment and self-esteem go hand in hand for ACODs. They believe that they were left as children because they were not worth loving. An ACOD who was twenty-one when her parents separated said she reacted like a five-year-old. She was at college when she got the word of her parents' divorce. She curled herself up on her bed and rocked herself, crying for mommy. "I couldn't understand. I felt abandoned and as if I belonged to no one."

This woman, now thirty, says that fear of abandonment is a daily issue for her. In relationships, she feels she is expendable. Because she feels expendable, she acts expendable. She is not able to communicate her needs to her partner, and she does not risk speaking things she believes will alienate him. Her partner then feels he cannot achieve intimacy with her, which is true. She is in control of the relationship and hiding from him her true needs and herself. How can he be intimate with someone he doesn't know?

Another ACOD said she "does her abandonment" in this way: "I set up the situation so that I leave my partner before he leaves me. Then I don't have to believe I was abandoned by him. I find that I throw away what I want most in the fear that it will leave anyway. I do this because I believe I don't deserve the things I want most."

In order to avoid abandonment, some ACODs go to extremes to maintain relationships that are dysfunctional. Many ACODs say they focus all their energy on trying to make sure their spouse or partner will not leave, that he or she will always be happy. These behaviors become overbearing to the person who is the recipient of them. They also result in the ACOD's losing all perspective about what is right and ethical in relationships.

One ACOD couple got themselves into a moral dilemma when they formed a business partnership with an older couple. They discovered that the older couple were falsifying records and receiving kickbacks from suppliers. The ACOD couple were aware that the activity was illegal and could endanger their enterprise. "Everything in me wanted to ignore what I was seeing," said the man. "I loved this older couple. They were like the parents I never had. The thought of their abandoning us was terrifying to me." The ACOD couple did confront the older couple. Although the confrontation was not pleasant, it taught the ACODs a lot about their illusions. Fearing abandonment, they refused to see their business partners for who they really were. They made them into the parents they wanted. When they saw that they were prepared to lie and cheat to maintain their illusion and stave off abandonment, they realized how far gone they were. "This experience really woke us up," continued the man. "It showed us we could see people for who they are, and it taught us that to go along with dishonesty meant we would ultimately abandon ourselves and our own integrity."

Inability to work through the abandonment paradigm leaves ACODs miserable. They end up repeating many of the mistakes of their parents. They do exactly what they swore they would never do. Many ACODs agree that they recreate the same scenario as their parents' divorce in all relationships. They are alternately the "good guy" or the "victim." They do not know there might be healthy ways to end a relationship.

While most of our focus has been abandonment in relationships, there is a deeper level to this issue. All of the examples I have considered have one thing in common. In order to accommodate others, control relationships, and leave partners before they leave, ACODs have first to abandon themselves. This means that ACODs do not focus on their feelings, their awareness, or their needs. In many cases, ACODs do not even know their needs because the divorce process was so all-encompassing it became their sole focus. In other cases, ACODs knew they had needs, but they deliberately set them aside in order to maintain control of a relationship. Thus, the oppression ACODs experience in the abandonment of divorce is internalized by them. Where once, as children, they were abandoned by caretakers, now as adults they do it to themselves. Many ACODs attest to this fact: being left by others was not nearly as destructive as abandoning themselves.

"Abandoning themselves" means ACODs shut down their awareness. Whether because they believe they are worthless or because it is too painful to feel, they do not consider their perceptions valid. ACODs accept other people's assessment of the situation. This is a deadening process and leaves them at the whim of outside forces. If you can't trust yourself, whom can you trust?

Rarely has an ACOD recovered who has not faced the issue of abandonment. It is central to developing a solid inner core and reestablishing an authentic sense of self-worth.

6. ACODs Have Difficulty Setting Limits and Personal Boundaries

As ACODs work with the effects of divorce on their lives, they appreciate their vulnerability. This is borne out in their struggle to set appropriate boundaries. The antagonism that existed between parents was a stressor that affected ACODs for years. In many cases, their parents' hostility went on long after the divorce was finalized. Children listened to their parents' complaining about one another in front of them, suffered through their enlisting their children as spies, watched as they renegotiated custody agreements. It was difficult, if not impossible, not to be pulled into those scenes. Boundary problems always have to do with knowing where we end and someone else begins. In the dysfunctional family, the lines are blurred and sometimes nonexistent. Consequently, many ACODs carry a sense of being used into their adult life.

ACODs felt used in various ways, some of which guide their relationships with others in later life. A woman ACOD who felt she was both the brunt of her parents' aggression and a sounding board for her mother now continues her "sounding board" role in her office. Everybody shares their troubles with her. She spends hours on the phone after work calling co-workers to check on them, express her concern, etc. She is also a doormat and readily takes on work others refuse. She has simply transferred her pattern from her family of origin to her work community.

ACODs may live out inappropriate roles given to them by their parents. This was the case with one young woman who feels she was used by her mother to meet the mother's emotional needs. The mother related to her daughter, aged ten, as if she were an adult. Instead of seeking support from caring friends and family, the mother isolated herself and expected her main support to come from her daughter. This later extended to the mother's flirting with the daughter's boyfriends. The daughter received mixed messages from the mother that she was to live the mother's unfulfilled dreams for a career, as well as sustain a successful marriage. The young woman entered adulthood not sure what she wanted for her own life, and with a sense of dread that she could not possibly be what her mother expected.

Another ACOD says he is aware of the trouble he has in setting limits. He usually feels suspicious that he may be used and avoids being vulnerable to protect himself against having others care for him. His problem reverberates in ACOD circles.

ACODs operate dualistically. They either disappear totally into others, or they establish a thick wall so no one gets in. Both behaviors are dysfunctional. This problem extends to almost every area of their lives.

A thirty-year-old ACOD grinned when he told me that he still has a hard time knowing when someone is teasing him in a gentle way or being mean. Another ACOD pondered the fact that she is inherently a nurturing person. She enjoys giving, but she is often suspicious of others' motives. Are they using me? Will others think I'll always be this generous and come to expect this from me?

A woman who went from being used by her mother in a prolonged and bitter custody battle to a fundamentalist Christian husband observed, "One can only be used if one lets that happen. But how do you fight such powerful people as your mother, your husband, and the teachings of the church that you are to be submissive as a wife?"

The problem of letting oneself be used frequently shows up in the workplace. Many ACODs say they stay overtime, take disagreeable tasks, put up with hostile supervisors. "I thought hostile people were normal," said a forty-year-old man with a laugh. "I had seen so much hostility in my family. I just put up with it at work." This same man said something I heard from many ACODs. "I never knew my boundaries. I don't know the boundaries of others. I feel afraid that if I refuse to be used, I will be abandoned."

A forty-five-year-old ACOD whose parents divorced when he was eleven told me that his life was a series of violated boundaries. They were strung out behind him like a railroad track. Jerry said that he did feel responsible for his parents' divorce, even though he was told he was not. "I had needs as a kid and I don't remember anyone asking me what I needed or how the divorce affected me. So I just screwed up my little face and determined to take care of myself and my parents both."

As an adult, Jerry's latest episode with unclear boundaries almost cost him his job. He was part of a business situation in which a department needed a "fall guy" to blame for the failure of a project. At a high-level meeting, Jerry was identified as the sole culprit. Although Jerry was partially responsible for the failure (others had been involved), he neither defended himself nor described the roles others had played. "I sat there and took it. I knew it was wrong. I knew I was being used, but I was terrified about what would happen if I spoke up. I believed my coworkers would reject me, so I kept my mouth shut."

ACODs are hard on themselves, and they set up situations in which they allow other people to perpetuate abuse. Many ACODs simply do not recognize the fact that they are being used. If their childhood experiences and models were of adults invading their space and making their troubles their children's, they tend to believe that such activity is normal. An ACOD who lost her boundaries in relation to her mother got the message from her father that something was "wrong" with her mother, and hence with her. She tried to be especially good, loving, kind, smart, courteous, trustworthy, and uncomplaining because if she was not, it would be a reflection on her mom, and that was unbearable.

There are several dimensions to setting limits as ACODs become older. One is setting limits in relationship to others. The other is setting limits in relationship to themselves. In setting limits with others, ACODs first need to learn when they are being used by others, and then they must learn to tell people to stop using them. Many ACODs have learned to tell when they are being used, but they do not tell the other to stop—as in the example of the man who watched himself be used as the "fall guy." Sometimes, ACODs avoid facing the complexity of confronting other people by simply setting stringent boundaries that keep everybody away. This tactic may work with casual acquaintances, but it is deadly with spouses, partners, and children. A female ACOD told me that she continued to have trouble setting limits in rearing her son. She believes his inability to grow up is probably related to this shortcoming in her.

The second area is setting limits for themselves. Several ACODs relate that they became utterly compulsive in relation to food and money. Others say they leapt into exciting relationships, only to be hurt time and again. Their view of what they need becomes distorted, and they seek things and persons that actually prevent them from gaining a true sense of themselves.

ACODs may live so detached from their experience and their needs that they set unrealistic limits, limits disrespectful of themselves. Letting themselves be invaded by others, or finding themselves taking others over, lowers self-esteem. ACODs have low self-esteem to begin with, and recurrent depression often accompanies a lack of boundaries. Many ACODs agree that they are angry about being used, but anger is too scary to risk. Instead, they become depressed, as would be expected of those who let themselves be the world's doormat.

An ACOD woman said at the end of her long interview with me, "I believe that this issue of boundaries was the key issue I had to face to recover from my parents' divorce process. Once it was addressed, I feel I had a firm footing to deal with a lot of my other ACOD patterns." She was right. As she dealt with setting limits and personal boundaries, she regained a sense of self, a self that she carried with her into all her other efforts at recovery.

7. ACODs Feel Helpless

ACODs' feelings of helplessness go back to a single event. They were powerless to stop the breakup of their parents' marriage and the fragmenting of their families. ACODs express their sense of helplessness over and over in their stories. John, whom we met earlier, said, "I had this dreadful feeling in the pit of my stomach that my mom and dad were going to split and there was just nothing I could do to stop it. It felt like a tornado. I knew it was going to touch down. I just didn't know when or where."

Indeed, ACODs feel caught up in the inevitability of divorce. They feel tossed around by divorce's events. Around this characteristic of helplessness, it becomes strikingly clear that parents are separate from their children and will not always make decisions that please children. In response to helplessness, ACOD children acted out to get attention, became little helpers to ease the pain, or got busy taking responsibility. In the end, their efforts did not change anything.

As adults, helplessness is manifested in three ways. First, ACODs often do not know how to respond in various situations. Second, they stand by watching in situations where they should act, and third, they lack some communication and social skills. All three of these aspects of helplessness are related to the fact that as children, some developmental needs were put on hold during the divorce process. Depending upon one's age and place in the family, ACODs may have more or less difficulty with this characteristic. For example, an ACOD who was the firstborn and a hero child in her family has few of these helpless characteristics. She swung into action and became a little parent to four siblings. However, the four younger siblings feel helpless much of the time and avoid most social situations.

ACODs do not know how to respond in various situations and express this in a variety of ways. One woman is aware she does not respond appropriately, so she does extensive research before she enters a situation. Often, she overprepares. An advertising executive, she checks out situations such as company retreats by asking others what kind of clothes they will wear, how much should she be prepared to bring in the way of files and charts. Or there is an architect whose boss accused him of overdesigning, playing it extra safe, and using more materials than were necessary. Another woman whose helplessness has plagued her all her life says that her inability to respond was so painful to her that she escaped geographically, moving to another city and taking another job. She knew it was a temporary fix and that it only took her attention away from the basic problem for a while. As this woman reflected on her childhood, she recalled that as her parents were divorcing, she did not experience any strong emotion coming from them. "Both Mom and Dad were very controlled. I knew they were under great stress, yet they showed no feelings. They were so flat affectively that they responded the same at a funeral as at a birthday party. I believe their lack of emotion brought on the divorce. Unfortunately for me, I knew there were appropriate ways to respond to people. I just didn't learn what they were."

Often, ACODs stand by watching in situations where they should act. Many ACODS remember how helpless they felt in the face of physical violence in their homes. Sometimes, their own safety depended upon their being quiet or becoming invisible. Many ACODs who were also incest victims know this characteristic well. Their very safety depended upon passivity. Several ACODs say they feared the hostility of their parents and learned to become invisible and small so the anger would not be directed toward them. Often, standing by and not knowing what to do stems from having poor role models. Children studied adults for how to act and respond, and they saw victims and aggressors, or passive people pretending nothing was wrong.

A woman who taught in a Midwest high school said she experienced the consequences of her passivity in her job. In going through a student's homework papers, she found a sheet inadvertently included. It was a note to one student from another about taking money from the cold-drink machines. She held on to the sheet for two weeks, all the while listening to a stream of messages going through her mind: "It's not my business." "It's probably nothing." "I have no proof." "I'll get someone in trouble." Still, she felt uneasy because she knew a group had vandalized the school office and there was great concern about their activities. She remained isolated and did not seek support or advice from anyone. The situation reached a crisis when the physical education office was broken into and equipment was stolen. At this point, the woman delivered the note. Indeed, it led to a gang that operated in the neighborhood surrounding the school.

In discussing this event and her response, the woman said, "I know intellectually what I should have done, yet emotionally, I felt frozen in denial and passivity. And I felt five years old again, and any action on my part felt like a risk." This woman went on to describe her family, which during the divorce process had become chaotic and fearful. When she expressed her needs in that setting, she was angrily told to grow up and that her needs were "stupid." She was five at the time of the divorce. At that time, and for the rest of her life, she says she became accustomed to suppressing her thoughts, feelings, and disagreements.

ACODs lack some communication and social skills. ACODs are probably not much different from the rest of the world in this. Communication and social skills seem to be in short supply! Again, ACODs' deficits in this area go back to what they learned in their families and what they saw modeled. Before the divorce, and during it, their parents' focus was on getting through a hard period. After the divorce, the custodial parent was probably too busy working and parenting to attend to communication and social needs. Also, some ACODs may have shut down emotionally and developmentally. They were not open to learning.

Many ACODs say their biggest communication problems are in the area of intimate relationships. Some say it scares them even to ask, "What is a relationship? How do you communicate in one?" Others find that communication about feelings of anger, sorrow, and fear is extremely difficult. Several ACODs say they expect people to read their minds. In that way, they do not have to expend the effort to ask for what they need. Nor do they have to risk being rejected. Another ACOD says, "I can't get the right words to come out. I am very shy, and have been since my parents' divorce. I thought my way through most situations and wouldn't risk saying anything for fear it would come out wrong."

A successful physician reflected that he felt burdened all his teen years by his parents' split. Yet, he never asked them to leave him out of their squabbles, and it never occurred to them that he might be troubled by being drawn in. Consequently, as an adult, he feels that most contacts are like a burden to him. Today, he describes himself thus: "As for my patients, I wish they would push their problems into a slot. Then I'd develop their treatment plan and push the solution back out through the slot. I dislike face-to-face contact, and I feel burdened by their illness."

At work and in intimate relationships, ACOD patterns abound. Such simple things as communicating needs, asking for what they want, and knowing what they want are hard for ACODs. Some have recognized their deficiencies in these areas and have set out to learn skills in communication. Others have sought therapy to remove the blocks to intimacy and to deal with their helplessness. It is always obvious when ACODs are beginning to heal from these issues: they regain their voices. They begin to speak up and stand up for what they want. It is a risk and it is necessary. Helplessness was learned in some divorcing families, and ACODs can unlearn it as they heal.

8. ACODs Seek a Home and Economic Security

"Home" is a word laden with emotion for ACODs, and it carries multiple meanings. For many ACODs, it means a safe place, a place where they are protected from the stresses of life and where they keep their things. It is an actual place, a structure, and it is full of the familiar.

For other ACODs, "home" is people, sometimes family members, sometimes friends, or both. Home is a community of people who welcome us exactly as we are. It is an environment where ACODs are known and loved, where they do not have to pretend.

Finally, home is inside a person. It is a feeling of comfort with oneself, as in the phrase, "I'm at home with myself."

ACODs use all of these descriptions of home, sometimes interchangeably, and they have strong feelings about this issue. For most of them, home was the most visible thing that changed when their parents divorced. When divorce broke apart what they had come to know and trust as home, many ACODs could never recapture a feeling of "home" in any other place. Where joint custody was arranged, children had two residences. In the best of these cases, they thought they were lucky to have two homes. Sometimes, though, neither place felt like a real home.

As a result of the inexplicable loss of home in divorce, ACODs feel anchorless. They go to extraordinary measures to create a home. Sometimes the things ACODs do continue their dysfunctional behavior. One ACOD says she tries to find a "home" in relationships with men. She latches on to a man and wants to make it work, no matter how hopeless it is. Another ACOD says he will tolerate inappropriate behavior from his family far beyond the point where others would call a halt, so fearful is he that he will lose his only home. Other ACODs become whirling dervishes of domestic activity. One ACOD described herself as a "human doing" rather than a human being. She wants to be a good wife, a gourmet cook, a perfect helpmate, as if she can make up for what she lost as a child.

A forty-year-old woman who describes herself as "extremely domestic" says she learned from others how to make a home "homey," because she never learned that as a child. Despite her efforts, her house doesn't feel safe and happy to her. She wonders if "homey" is window dressing, and if she has deeper issues to resolve before she will feel "at home" in any place.

Some ACODs long to settle down in one place for a while, but find they uproot frequently. They go from place to place, never having the home they want. Many consider three years in one place a long time. ACODs were transient as children; they are transient as adults.

It is interesting to note that those ACODs who spent time in foster homes, or who had multiple dwellings as children, are those most adamant that home is inside them. One thirty-eight-year-old man said that the very concept of home is strange to him. He never had a home in the traditional sense. To him, home is within himself, or in time spent with his twin brother. An ACOD who was put in an orphanage at age thirteen often said, "Wherever I am is home," and bravely rationalized her transient lifestyle. Although she does feel at home inside herself, she saw that she needed more and is now proud that she has finally created a home for herself in her residence.

Similarly, economic security is a source of constant anxiety for ACODs. The majority of divorcing families experienced a reduction in financial security as a result of the divorce. Research reported by Prof. Lenore Weitzman of Harvard University shows that, on the average, women with children undergo a 73 percent decline in their standard of living immediately after the divorce, while their ex-husband's standard of living increases by 42 percent.[1] If this economic trend continues, we will face a lopsided, gender-related, two-class society where women and children do not fare well in comparison to men.

A twenty-nine-year-old ACOD shared a story typical of many:

> From the time I was young, I had the horrible image of my parents' calling my brother and me and saying, "We are divorcing." That exact scenario happened. Then we never heard another word about it for six years, which is when the actual divorce took place.

My father was a manufacturer's rep and he made a lot of money. We lived in a beautiful house and my father flew his own plane and drove a Mercedes. Over the six years of my parents' separating, my father became progressively weirder. He had insisted my mother stay at home to raise us kids. My mother was very bright and she poured all her effort into being the perfect wife. Consequently, she had no marketable skills when the divorce occurred.

My father sold all his assets and put them in Swiss banks where my mother could not get to them. He bought a yacht and sailed away. Within a month, we went from "fat city" to living in dire poverty. I had been in private schools; now I attended public schools. The largest material hurt I experienced was that I could not go to the college of my choice. My father said he would go to jail before he would pay for college. To this day, I refuse to admit my standard of living has decreased. My income is at poverty level, yet I have built up such debts that I attend Debtors Anonymous.

As parents established their own lifestyles after the divorce, children felt the effects of their different economic realities. A woman remembers going back and forth between her parents' separate households as economically "schizophrenic." Her mother was awarded her custody, and they lived at a subsistence level. Her father had penthouses, limousines, and airplanes. He showered her with frivolous gifts when she visited him. Then she returned to her mother's home, where they had barely enough to eat. "He bought me dresses that cost more than our food budget for the month. As I got older, I saved the tags and returned the clothes to get money for my mother and me."

Most ACODs have had to deal with fathers who pay little or nothing toward child support, and it is a rare father who pays a child's college expenses. The research bears this out. After their children reach the age of eighteen, even wealthy fathers do not want further financial responsibility for them. This means that thousands of children of divorce are putting themselves through college without eligibility for student aid because they have at least one parent with ample financial resources, although that parent is unwilling to pay the bill.

The financial situation of children does not necessarily improve in families with a stepparent. Margie, an attractive eighteen-year-old, shared with me a situation I heard repeatedly from ACODs. Margie's parents divorced when she was seven, and she remained with her mother, who remarried. As part of the divorce settlement, her biological father agreed to pay her college expenses, but he reneged when it came time. Margie's stepfather did not believe it was his responsibility to foot the bill, and her mother did not have the necessary resources. Both her biological father and her stepfamily were affluent, yet as Margie observed, "I was parent rich and penny poor. Sometimes I felt like I fell between the cracks in this divorce. No one really cared and I was just an expense nobody wanted."

ACODs have fears about whether they can really make it on their own financially. For some, money was used as a manipulative tool, so it often seemed scarce. They found themselves playing games and fighting to hold a parent to an agreement. ACODs picked up a scarcity mentality as they observed fathers complaining about the demands on them or disappearing altogether, and mothers struggling to make ends meet. For some ACODs, economic considerations rule their lives. They are conscious of the need for money for necessities, but they tend to spend on frivolities instead.

ACODs take steps to compensate for what happened to them as children. One woman says she has to look affluent even though she has little money because she felt so "poor looking" after her parents' divorce. Consequently, she buys expensive-looking clothes and attends social activities where the affluent hang out. An ACOD deliberately took a job in investment banking because he wanted a job that would insure a good income and massive savings. In his family of origin, they met their basic needs but there was never extra. He is determined not to repeat that experience, yet he is not sure that investment banking is his true vocation. It just keeps the "wolf away from the door."

Obviously, not all ACOD issues are internal or psychological. They are also material. An an early age, many ACODs had to deal with shifting economies in the home. These experiences continue to affect them deeply. Where ACODs live, how they live, if they buy or rent, if they have a garden, what job they accept, what they think of as home, and whom they consider to be family are questions ACODs carry through adulthood. Coming home to themselves is an essential task for every ACOD, as is dealing with the material world in a healthy way. To be balanced in healing, ACODs need to face both their material and psychological issues, and to come to grips with their past in their present choices.

9. ACODs Idealize and Blame Parents and Other Authority Figures

It seems inevitable that everyone in our society has to work through his or her feelings about parents. Can this characteristic be so different for ACODs? ACODs do share the need to deal with parental issues, and for ACODs these issues are distinctive, recurring, and related to the experience of their parents' divorce.

A large issue for ACODs is their different relationship to fathers and mothers. Although more fathers are requesting custody and receiving it, and joint custody is popular, the fact remains that in 90 percent of all divorces, children live with their mothers as the custodial parent. As a result, ACODs simply do not know their fathers, especially if the divorce took place when children were very young. ACODs may have almost no memory of their fathers. An ACOD whose father left when she was three says, "My father was a handsome visitor who came to bring a gift at Christmas, Easter, and my birthday. He did not know me and I did not know him." The experience with fathers varies from ACODs whose fathers disappeared or were seen only a few times over many years, to those who had regular, ongoing contact.

Some children gravitated to their fathers. They seemed more relaxed and emotionally available than mothers, who were overworked and overwhelmed by their newly single state. In some cases, fathers raised children and ACODs have maintained solid relationships with them. Nevertheless, the majority of ACODs feel estranged from their fathers.

This estrangement takes several forms. ACODs have a hard time understanding why a parent would leave them financially stranded, as many fathers did. Fathers' anger toward mothers sometimes flowed over to the children. This was the case for the ACOD whose father left his entire estate to his own sisters and brothers so that it would not go to his ex-wife's daughter, his only child. Said this woman, "I never understood why I should be punished. It's my mother he divorced, not me."

In other instances, time with fathers was superficial, at holidays and on weekends. ACODs had no opportunity to see them in the entire range of their moods or lives. ACODs carry a lot of pain about the unavailability of their fathers. Male ACODs are wistful about their fathers, and angry. A thirty-six-year-old, whose father left when he was thirteen, remembers his rage that his father never had time for him before or after the divorce. The father remarried soon after the divorce and was busy establishing a new family. "I felt so bewildered that my dad had all this energy to bounce a new baby on his knee, but he couldn't be there for me, especially as I became a man and really needed a man in my life. I truly did not know my dad. I longed to understand what made him tick the way he did."

The desire to know their fathers is a common theme among ACODs. Well into adulthood, ACODs have the urge to understand these men who were a part of their lives and then went away, either entirely or gradually. Many ACODs believe information about their fathers would ease the pain. A little information can prove frustrating, however. As one ACOD said, "Every time I learn something about my father, he changes, so I end up wondering who is he, after all?"

Mothers are another case altogether. Many ACODs struggle with dependency in their dynamics with their mothers. The dependency goes both ways. Some ACODs felt dependent upon their mothers and still do. Some mothers became dependent on ACODs as children and still are. As adults, ACODs may feel guilty leaving their mothers.

Immediately after the divorce, several ACODs experienced their mothers' forming bonds with them that felt unhealthy. They were told they would have to take on more responsibility, that they were all their mothers had to count on. An ACOD who married at twenty said her mother did everything in her power to convince her daughter that her daughter's marriage would not work, *and* who was going to help her out if she let her daughter marry? This ACOD said she felt utterly controlled by her mother. She married anyway, although she experienced guilt for years.

Many ACODs speak of the difficulties they had in going to college or moving out on their own. They worried excessively about their mothers. If they were the last child to leave, they sometimes postponed the move for several years. Even in cases where mothers insisted they would be fine on their own, young adult children felt tied into caretaking roles.

Some ACODs had exceptional mothers. They supported their children without acting like martyrs. Several ACODs express admiration for mothers who kept families together single-handedly. A young man who is twenty-five and just starting out on his own career spoke admiringly of his mother. He said, "When I see all that goes into supporting a family financially and emotionally, I really am astounded at what my mom did after the divorce. She was fantastic. I'm not one of these ACODs who feels like I have to stay around to take care of her. In fact," he said, laughing, "I'd kind of like to stay around so she'll take care of me!"

Like fathers, mothers were sometimes emotionally unavailable to their children after the divorce. They were tired after working all day. They had the stress of single parenting. They were rebuilding their social networks, entering new marriages. Children may have found themselves with other caretakers over long periods, or being sent to relatives. As children took on increased responsibility, they were not asking for what they needed. Often, they did not know what they needed. They felt empty and unloved and they may continue with those feelings into adulthood.

A surprising number of ACODs created myths about their noncustodial parent that served to perpetuate the illusions about this parent. Fathers were more often the subjects of these favorable myths because they were absent more than mothers. Mothers seem to receive more criticism than fathers, who were idealized. Even when the actual experience was of a harsh, selfish, and irresponsible parent, ACODs chose to ignore that information and see that parent as warm, generous, and caring. When they could not deny a parent's shortcomings, they created an elaborate rationale to justify the behavior. Often, ACODs excused one parent's behavior by blaming the other parent. ("He would never have been violent if my mother hadn't pushed him so hard.")

A twenty-five-year-old ACOD who was a gifted musician, the winner of numerous music competitions, but who attended a little-known college because he had to support himself completely, adamantly defended his father as being unable to contribute to his college education. The ACOD insisted his father's refusal to help was due to the enormous debts incurred in the divorce process. In actuality, the father's after-tax income amounted to $95,000 a year, a fact the son refused to acknowledge, so great was his need to protect his father and himself from the disappointment of seeing his father as a man who had intentionally separated himself from the financial and emotional support of his son.

ACODs' experience with their parents through the divorce process can follow them all through their lives. It is manifest in the fact that ACODs refuse to see their parents and authority figures for who they really are. They often expect from authority figures things they never received from parents—unconditional love and acceptance. Many ACODs have had to work hard on their relationships with bosses and others in authority positions. They may find themselves enraged with authorities, then discover it is not authorities with whom they are angry. It is their parents. Or they may find themselves throwing themselves wholeheartedly into a work situation, making it their whole life because they receive such adulation from a boss. ACODs work themselves to death in the pursuit of praise, not because they inherently like the job.

Frequently, ACODs' stance toward parents and authorities is dualistic: ACODs idealize them and blame them. Many ACODs used this dualism in relation to parents. Dad could do no wrong, mother was terrible, or the reverse. These positions would shift as they developed, but the basic process of idealization or blame was the same.

Marilyn is an ACOD whose parents became psychologically abusive during the divorce process. Her mother would promise her toys, which she would buy. At the last minute, she would return the items, claiming that she couldn't afford the toys because of the divorce. Marilyn's father stood by during this behavior, neither condoning it nor objecting. "I felt beat up by her cruelty and his silence," she said. Nevertheless, Marilyn is astounded at how she still protects her parents in her mind. "I make excuses for them like 'they must have been so distraught' or 'they really didn't know what they were doing to me.' I really refuse to acknowledge their responsibility for my treatment," she concluded. Now an adult, Marilyn displaces her rage on authority figures. At work, people give her a wide berth. Supervisors report that she is moody and unwilling to take on usual tasks. She has been known to throw tantrums and to respond cynically when addressed by authorities. Needless to say, she does not keep a job for long.

Another ACOD spent the first fifteen years of her adult life blaming her parents and idealizing those in authority. After extensive therapy, she realized neither her parents nor her bosses deserved such treatment. This woman discovered that she could see her mother and her father as individual persons. They were not categories of "Moms should be and do . . . Dads should be and do."

ACODs' confusion about parents and authorities frequently extends to all adults. About half say that even now they don't trust adults. Trust does not come easily for ACODs. They found their trust violated in their divorcing families as those they thought they could trust left, physically or emotionally. ACODs express this caution in various ways. Some examine others carefully to see if they warrant trust. They are questioned extensively. Others feel they are being interrogated. Some ACODs trust men but not women, or women and not men. ACODs usually have a few trusted friends, but not many. Some ACODs confess that they do not see themselves as trustworthy, and this has made it nearly impossible to trust others. Then there is the twenty-six-year-old woman who says, "I find I want to trust everyone, so I confide in them from the beginning, and I feel hurt and let down when my trust in them is broken." Her paradox is that she wants to trust everyone, but she doesn't trust anyone.

Whether ACODs idealize or blame, the outcome is the same: They do not see their parents for who they are. ACODs keep themselves busy with the illusion by making parents into something else. On the blame side of the dualism, they seek the one to accuse for a failed marriage and a broken family. This process of seeking someone to blame is exhausting. ACODs fail to see that when they blame or idealize, they move away from taking responsibility for their own feelings. Sometimes, there are not easy answers for childhood experiences. They cannot control how parents behaved and they can feel their own pain around their relationship with parents.

As adults, ACODs need to confront the issue of seeing people exactly as they are. The longer they persist in living in an illusion, the more their life process bogs down. A phrase I heard a lot from ACODs is "my parents did the best they knew how." It is important not to use that phrase to avoid the pain of divorce. Sometimes parents did not do the best they knew how. They may have been reacting blindly to their own dysfunctional past, and taking it out on children. They, too, could be victims of their heritage. One ACOD revealed the intense frustration of this vicious cycle when he said, "The kids end up divorcing the parents just to survive." Regardless of how terrible or wonderful their families were, ACODs still have the task of living honestly in the truth of their past. Trust is not possible where illusion prevails.

10. ACODs Have Unrealistic Expectations for Their Relationships and Marriages

Unless ACODs become hermits, they cannot avoid relationships. Consequently, issues with intimacy are usually triggered in every relationship ACODs establish. They have unrealistic expectations for relationships and marriages. So many of them say, "I don't want to repeat my parents' mistakes." ACODs almost certainly will repeat them if they do not face their relationship issues. Several themes characterize the ACOD approach to relationships. Facing them is the beginning of change.

ACODs guess at what normal families, relationships, and intimacy are. This tendency is similar to that experienced by adult children of addictive and dysfunctional families. They, too, guess at what "normal" is. They have defined their dysfunction as their only reality for so long, they believe it is the norm for all functioning. Similarly, ACODs have the experience of immersion in families that operated as a closed system. Their family systems operated with tunnel vision. Children were mired in their family's experience and did not look outside it. This experience stifled children, took a lot of time and attention, and prevented them from learning new behaviors. Divorcing families became children's only reality, and they had no touchstone for other ways of operating.

One woman relates that their family secret was just how devastating the divorce was. As a girl, she felt she would betray her family were she to talk about her experience. This silence kept her from intimacy with others. She always needed to look as if she were "fine."

Keeping the family secret and looking fine perpetuated the dysfunction. It prevented children from asking for help and learning from others. When ACODs surreptitiously looked around to figure out how such important life experiences as relationships and intimacy were handled, they turned to television, movies, and their own fantasies to guide them and help them to set standards. This led to a certain rigidity in thinking. They believed everyone else's family was normal, and they were different. It was a surprise for many ACODs to discover that others also suffered in silence. Many grew up practicing a lot of impression management!

Children of divorce felt separate from their peers. Those whose parents divorced prior to the 1970s, when divorce became the choice of 50 percent of all married people, felt shameful and out of place with friends from intact families.

A forty-year-old ACOD was the only child of a minister and his wife. They lived in a small town in a religiously and politically conservative area. When Carol told me her story, she was wide-eyed with remembrance of the events surrounding the divorce. She said, "My mother initiated the divorce. Fortunately, the predivorce process was only six months, but it felt like an eternity. In that town, being the minister's wife, my mother was looked upon as a whore or a devil. I somehow was an extension of her. My father, the minister, mouthed Christian platitudes, but he did nothing to prevent the shame that was directed our way. Almost overnight I lost my playmates, as no one was allowed to associate with me. I felt like an outcast. There was no way my mother and I could remain in that town, even though my mother had been born there. We literally left in the dark of night and I've never returned, so painful are my memories."

The social stigma surrounding divorce survives, leaving many feeling uneasy, even today. One ACOD echoes many others: "I've always felt like I never quite met up to the rest of the world, that I was deficient somewhere. I acted like someone standing on the fringes of the crowd." In addition, ACODs did not always invest very heavily in establishing peer relationships because they were so caught up in their family system.

Probably no area of life is more troublesome for ACODs than relationships. The majority of ACODs had poor modeling when it came to relationships. Parents, in many cases, related through aggression, secrecy, and power plays. Personal boundaries were transgressed. ACODs knew something was wrong with that style of relating, and that it was all they knew. The alternatives were not obvious. Consequently, they struggle with relationships. Occasionally, ACODs make the choice not to risk intimacy at all.

Many find they are attracted to people who are not available for relationships. An ACOD who admitted she didn't know what a healthy relationship was lived a pattern of jumping from man to man. She sought instant intimacy. She believed she would get into the relationships as part of a blackout. Then she would wake up weeks later, wondering, "What the hell am I doing here?"

ACODs disappear into the needs of others. One ACOD writes that he survived his parents' split by mirroring back to them what they needed to see and hear. This left him lost and invisible in his relationships, and he felt resentful that his own needs were not met. This man finds that he attracts people to himself who are like his parents, who are going through the same things his parents went through. "I then get overly involved trying to help them not make the same mistakes." As he learns to have a self and be more visible, he learns it is acceptable to be seen and heard. He does not have to hide to survive.

ACODs face marriage and other commitments carrying the same anxiety with which they meet relationships. Here again we see the characteristic ACOD dualism. Among some, the attitude is, "Marriage is no big deal. If I don't like it, I'll leave." The other attitude is, "This marriage has to last forever. I will not take the risk to marry unless I am certain it will last."

There are some data to suggest that ACODs are more likely to divorce than are persons whose parents had intact marriages. Several theories strive to explain why this would be so.[2] One study indicates that ACODs tend to marry at an earlier age than children from intact families. They leap into relationships that offer a way out of their dysfunctional families. ACODs gravitate into situations that are familiar, if dysfunctional, seeking a quick fix for their pain and a way to belong.

A third explanation is that ACODs feel a lower commitment to marriage to begin with. They do not have high expectations that marriage will work, so they do not give themselves fully to the process. This is the "if I don't like it, I'll leave" attitude described earlier.

A fourth explanation is that ACODs embark upon marriage and commitment with little sense of themselves and weak skills for relationship building. Several ACODs reveal that they expected their partners to meet all their needs. They had no concept of being responsible for their own needs. These persons clung to their partners, placing impossible burdens upon them to be everything. Of course, with such an assignment, their partners were certain to fail. The ACODs did not realize they needed to develop a support system to deal with the complexity of their needs.

Asking a partner to be everything is unrealistic. Asking a partner to be perfect is unrealistic. And asking partners to do for us things we will not do for ourselves is a setup for disaster. An ACOD who created a hopeless situation for herself did it this way. First, she entered marriage expecting it to make up for her miserable childhood. Then she waited for her partner to read her mind, and she attempted to do the same for him. When he did not know her desires or sense her moods intuitively, she felt hurt and removed herself from him in a silent pout. They only reunited when he eventually figured out her problem, or if he offered profuse apology (for something he didn't know he had done!). She then felt supported and emerged from her dark cloud. She felt much closer to her husband after he apologized. She believed this dynamic was healthy because, she reasoned, in her divorcing family, her father had never apologized. Variations of this behavior continued for five years, at which time her husband asked for a divorce. He said he felt he was the victim of mental cruelty in that he had to take responsibility for her moods as well as his own, and he was breaking down under her perfectionistic expectation of him as a mind reader. The ACOD was astonished because she felt good in the marriage, probably because she did not have to do anything in the relationship. Her husband had been doing the work for both of them.

Marriage and commitment are rarely solutions for all the issues ACODs carry. Commitment does not take away relationship problems, it can exacerbate them. Many ACODs have shared with me the fact that they feel considerable pain over their childhood experiences. ACODs have moved into relationships because they are kept busy and at the same time, out of touch with their pain. Marriage and commitment holds out the possibility of redeeming the past and doing better, where parents failed. Consequently, many ACODs make relationships their focus and commit to a relationship without making a prior commitment to themselves and their own recovery. ACODs have found that they need to develop a relationship with themselves, first. Until they make that primary and essential commitment, they are in no position to join with another. Unfortunately, most ACOD troubles stem from looking "out there" for someone (partner) or something (marriage) to fix them. Looking inside is step one. When they develop intimacy with themselves, they will be ready to relate to others and they will know how to ask for what they need.

THE
PROCESS
OF
HEALING

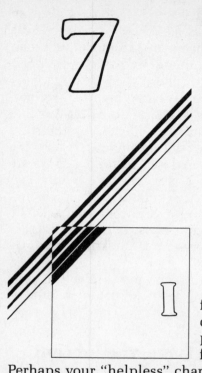

Recovering and Healing

7

I f you have identified with the characteristics of ACODs from the previous chapters, you may be feeling overwhelmed or hopeless. Perhaps your "helpless" characteristic has kicked in, and you are ready to abandon the search for healthier ways of relating. I encourage you to hang in there. The self-identification of ACOD characteristics is itself over half the battle. If you have seen yourself in some of the preceding situations and patterns, such naming can be scary, but it can also be a relief. Now it is time to go further and do something about how you feel and behave.

Before discussing specific resources for ACODs, I want to lay out some general considerations. These are overall principles that I believe need to be kept in mind as you recover from your ACOD experience.

Divorce Is a Process, Healing Is, Too

It is important to remember that you carry the ACOD characteristics because of a long process. You were not zapped in the night with a virus, to awake riddled with ACOD symptoms. There were periods of intensity and periods of slack in your divorcing family. The process lasted over time. Specific events of the divorce may now blur in your memory, but when you were in it, you were affected on a daily basis, even when you thought you were not being affected.

Healing is a process, too. I use the term "healing" deliberately. When the divorce process was dysfunctional, it was like a sickness or disease. Because you were affected by the sickness of dysfunctional divorce does not mean you are bad. We don't say we are bad when we come down with the flu. We are just sick. I think of our ACOD issues as a sickness to which you were vulnerable because your family immune system was not strong. Your resistance was down, and you were infected. The healing, then, is a process that continues. It would be grandiose to believe that any of us possesses a quick fix for family dysfunction.

You will need to go at your own pace and resolve issues as they come up. Each step heals, and you need patience. It takes time.

The Past Is Your Parents' Issue, the Present Is Your Issue

Blaming is cathartic, yet it is rarely productive. Spending inordinate amounts of time thinking "If only my parents had. . ." just keeps you stuck. Many ACODS have commented on how useless it is to wish things had been different. Some ACODs feel stalled by their parents' divorce. They return to that event as the beginning of all their troubles. They keep asking "Why?" as if having an answer would resolve something. This attitude gives you an excuse for not living your life.

In the course of working as a divorce and child-custody mediator and researching and writing this book, I have often wondered what was going on in the previous generations that so many adults knew so little about relationships and family. It is only hindsight that makes them appear deficient. Colleagues reminded me that this was the generation that endured the Great Depression, World War II, the Korean War, and Vietnam, all catastrophic events. This was the generation that had almost no access to therapy or self-help groups, and psychology was for "real crazies," and alcoholics were "weak willed." This was not the generation that knew how to ask for help, and when it did, little of value was available. Probably they tried to tough it out, and often they simply took out their frustrations on their families.

Regardless of what your parents did or did not do, you live your life in the present, and it is *your life*. Honoring your past and becoming honest about it are processes that aid your recovery. Ultimately, you must take responsibility for the life you have. Your focus needs to be on the present, not on "them" or the past.

Issues You Did Not Resolve as a Child, You Carry Into Adulthood

My colleague Dr. Anne Wilson Schaef has observed that the human system is ecology minded. We "recycle" our old material (she would say "our shit") over and over again until we deal with it. Then, it lets go, and we don't have to deal with it again. This is an important lesson for ACODs, and it should be an incentive to "clean up" your old issues.

You probably return with great frequency to all the events of the divorce, seeing there your loss of boundaries, your fear of intimacy, your excessive needs for control. These are old processes. They will plague you until you deal with them.

Your present gives you many opportunities to deal with your past through things called triggers. The way you know that you have old material to deal with is through these "triggers." Triggers are feelings or events in the present that bring up old, past material that you did not resolve when it happened. An example: A woman ACOD purchased a new home, and she and her family were preparing to move into it. Several days before moving, and on moving day itself, she was irritable, moody, and felt like hiding. She became excessively controlling and only added to her family's stress in moving. Fortunately, one of her friends observed to her, "Your reactions seem so out of proportion with the stress of moving, I wonder if something else is going on with you. Would you check it out?" The ACOD took some quiet time alone. She sat with her feelings, and soon, she had a flood of memories and sensations. She remembered that her divorcing family had changed residences frequently. Every move was filled with terror, a sense of loss, and a fear about meeting new people. Her present move was merely a trigger, reminding her that she had an old, unfinished process from childhood.

It is important in recovery that you see triggers for what they are. If the woman had focused on her present irritability, she would have missed the opportunity to work through a process from her past. That process would keep reappearing. Eventually, her family would just shrug and on subsequent moving days, say, "Mom always gets like this when we move," and Mom would inappropriately "dump" her moods on her family. Her family does not deserve this kind of abuse. It has nothing to do with them. When, however, she takes time to feel her old feelings and gain insight about the origin of her emotions, she is free to get on with her life without being triggered during subsequent moves.

Another example of triggers was related to me by a sixty-five-year-old woman. I think her story illustrates how long ACODs can hold on to the effects of divorce. Dorothy's parents separated when she was twelve. Although her father had gone away several times during the Depression to seek work, Dorothy always believed he would return. But at twelve, he left for good. Dorothy said, "I thought my father had left me, not my mother. I had always felt special and important in his eyes. When he left, my specialness was assailed. I believed my importance was in question if he could leave me."

As soon as she was able, Dorothy left home, got a job, and put herself through school. She eventually married and had several children. At the time of my conversation with her, Dorothy's husband had been dead for two years from a sudden stroke. She told me, "When my father left, I felt bad. I was a nobody. Since my husband's death, I feel that again. I feel I'm holding myself back. I feel my husband did the same to me as my father." Dorothy also told me that she has always argued with the men in her life. "I like men but I don't get along well with them. The effect of my parents' separation and divorce is that I decided you couldn't rely on a man to look after you, yet I wanted to have such a man in my life. My husband did look after me. Yet even with my good relationship with my husband, I didn't deal with my earlier sense of rejection by my father. When my father left, I felt undervalued by him and by society. When my husband died, I felt undervalued again and also undervalued by the society, which is such a couples society. I get desperately lonely and quite lost and confused. I don't know where I am."

Part of your recovery entails taking responsibility for your past and resolving your ACOD issues, so you don't make yourself and others miserable in the present. Triggers are actually gifts. They remind you that you have more work to do, and they give you the opportunity to do that work. A good clue that you are being triggered is that your reaction is out of proportion to the actual event. With the ACOD who feared moving, it would have been easy to dismiss her reaction as just the stress of moving. The key was that her reaction was much more intense than the situation warranted. This was obvious to her family and to her. They were giving her a wide berth. Overreacting is a good clue that there is an old process wanting attention. Once the ACOD entered into that old process and learned what she needed to learn, she could reenter the present moment with her family, make some apologies for her overbearing behavior, and get on with their move, feeling that she was going to a place where she had no reason for fear. She was, indeed, safe.

Dorothy's story shows that there is both a personal and a social component to the old feelings ACODs carry as the result of divorce. Her sense of herself as a valuable person was affected by losing her father and later triggered again in her husband's death and in the social discomfort she felt when she wasn't part of a couple. Rationally, Dorothy knows that her husband's death was not the same abandonment as her father's leaving. However, triggers aren't rational. They are about feelings. It is the old feeling that needs attention and that overwhelms Dorothy with each new loss.

ACODs Are Legion/You Are Not Alone

There are some ACODs who feel shame, guilt, and fear. They carry a stigma that I believe is societally induced. The stigma says there is something wrong with you because you came from a divorced family. The consequence of this attitude is that ACODs isolate from others and do not seek the help and support they need. They believe they are so unique that no one would understand their issues. This book is an attempt to counteract that thinking.

The fact is that ACODs are everywhere. In many areas, there are more ACODs than there are persons from intact families. It would be a mistake to believe that people from intact families have it all together. As will be seen later, the intact family itself may be one of the myths we hold on to in order to deny what is going on in families today. Dysfunction is everywhere in families. Divorce is only one manifestation of that dysfunction, and sometimes divorce is a healthy response to it.

Joining with others who share similar experiences has been proven to be one of the most effective modes of healing. Talking about your story, and hearing others' stories, helps you understand aspects of your past you would otherwise have missed. I remember the relief on a forty-six-year-old woman's face when she heard a young ACOD say that fighting was his primary way of achieving intimacy with his wife. He had learned it in his divorcing family, and it was also his behavior, and it was not working. Hearing his words helped the older woman realize that this was her attitude exactly. She began to understand the fighting/intimacy characteristic as a behavior inherited from her family that was dysfunctional for her now. She started to explore other ways of being in intimate relationships. Later, she told me that she had stayed so isolated with her ACOD history that she was not open to knowing there were others like her. She had been deeply relieved to discover she was not alone.

As you will see later, many of the resources for healing are self-help groups. I recommend this path to recovery because I believe that a group directly counteracts the isolation of the ACOD. Without addressing the isolation, ACODs live in their own worlds, believing those worlds are normal when in reality they are dysfunctional. ACODs learned isolation early. The divorcing family turns in on itself. The society tends to ignore it. Relatives keep their distance, not wanting to interfere. At the time of greatest need, the family is most alone. Consequently, sharing, talking, and hearing others' stories is a vital break with the past, ending isolation and providing an arena for learning and change.

Taking Responsibility for Yourself: Facing the ACOD Characteristics

As I travel around the United States, I notice a unique characteristic among Americans. I barely finish describing the ACOD experience when I sense a restlessness in the audience. Inevitably, the first question is, "What can I do about these things?" We Americans are not satisfied until we have *done* something. Then, we think it is solved. This penchant for action reminds me of some monks I know who went to a Tibetan Buddhist monastery to see how the monastic life was lived in Tibet. After a few days, the American monks approached the abbot and asked what chores they could perform to help out. The abbot looked incredulous. "My brothers," he said, "we don't *do* anything here. We just are." The monks slunk back to their chambers, newly aware that even in a lifestyle dedicated to prayer and solitude, they had fallen into the characteristic American mode of needing to be busy.

I think ACODs mistakenly believe that if they are not doing something, nothing is happening with their recovery from their ACOD characteristics, and of course, "doing" is an activity. But I believe there are many ways of healing from ACOD issues. Some of the ways are more active than others, and some have nothing to do with action.

The first step in your recovery is simply *naming* your experience. The reading of this book facilitates that process. It allows you to put a name on feelings and experiences you have carried for years, unaware of their significance. For many people, naming is a great relief. "Of course," they say, "*that's* what that is!" The naming makes the characteristics less powerful and less all-encompassing in your life. It cuts them down to size and puts them in perspective. In naming, it is important to decide which characteristics fit for you and which do not.

ACODs have found that once they have named or identified the characteristics they live with, they can begin to think, act, and feel differently. The important thing to remember is that you don't try to use naming as a way to get away from or escape a characteristic. Naming is not an escape; it is an act of honesty. Paradoxically, once you acknowledge that you take sides or feel abandoned or have difficulty setting limits, etc., you are on your way to interrupting those behaviors. When you remain in denial, you are captured by the characteristics of your ACOD history.

In the following pages, I restate the ACOD characteristics, then describe some ways ACODs who are healing have chosen to think or act in relation to those characteristics. My hope is that these examples will help guide you on your own road to recovery.

1. ACODs Have an Overdeveloped Sense of Responsibility

Instead of taking care of everyone else, looking out for their welfare and meeting their needs, recovering ACODs take responsibility for themselves. This is not as easy as it sounds. For one thing, you have spent more time learning about others than you have learning about yourself. You can readily get drawn into others' troubles because you are more practiced at helping than at sitting with yourself. Taking responsibility for yourself means giving yourself the time and space to know what you feel and what you need. Sometimes it means pulling back into yourself and checking in with yourself to see what you are feeling in a situation.

ACODs ought to be suspicious of excessive busyness, for this often keeps them away from doing their inner work, and they can use busyness to escape their feelings. An ACOD who became a little mother to four siblings after her parents' divorce said it is all she can do not to leap forward to volunteer for more tasks at her church. She receives a lot of affirmation for her efforts, affirmation she craves because she received so little of it from her family. Yet, she knows her excessive doing is a temporary fix for a hollowness she feels inside. When she takes responsibility for herself, when she nurtures herself, that void is lessened.

Taking self-responsibility is not selfishness. In fact, the best thing you can do for others is not to put the onerous burden of your caretaking on them, nor expect that they will do for you what you will not do for yourself. As you take responsibility for yourself, you learn about true caring, a caring that comes out of honesty and respect.

2. ACODs Attempt to Control Everything

The antidote to excessive controlling is simple, and not easy: *Let go!* Letting go occurs on several levels.

First, you need to realize that what you are dealing with is your illusion of control. You are deceived if you think that you can control at all. Surely, every ACOD had the early experience that they could not prevent their parents' divorce, no matter how good, how loving, how responsible they were. Your parents' decision to divorce had a life of its own. It went forward despite your efforts to control the outcome. So, you must first acknowledge and cope with the illusion that you can control. It is certainly difficult to let go of the illusion, if control is your thing!

At another level, ACODs need to ask themselves if they are willing to risk getting what they want. It is the experience of many ACODs that when they stop controlling and begin letting go, they often get what they want. This seems especially true in personal relationships. An ACOD described that, for years, she had tried every underhanded (i.e., controlling) way of getting her husband into therapy. She conveniently left the paper open to articles on therapy. She spoke glowingly of men she knew who were in therapy. She would indirectly say, "Have you ever been in therapy, or thought about it?" At some level, her husband felt her manipulation. She was trying to be controlling, but not getting what she wanted. As she faced her ACOD recovery, she began letting go, and one day, she spoke to her husband directly, and vulnerably, about what she wanted. She said, "I think our marriage is in trouble. I'm trying to take responsibility for myself and my part in our troubles. I wish you would take your part. I believe therapy could help both of us. I wish you'd consider it. It would mean a lot to me, but I know it is your decision, and I respect that it is." Then, she truly let go. She didn't nag him with reminders or watch his actions. And two weeks later, her husband was in therapy. As the woman reflected on this incident, she described it as one in which she felt good about whatever happened, regardless of the actual outcome. "I was thrilled that he finally got into therapy, but if he had not, I still felt good because I believe I was truly myself, and honest in our interaction. It was clear, and I did not feel the pull of my control."

It is risky to give up the illusion of control, but the consequences of staying in your control are an even greater risk. Those who control are trying to be little gods, and they find that since the human is not designed to be a god, they are frequently up against failure and frustration. Also, control takes a toll on your body. Perhaps ACODs take the ultimate leap of faith when they give up the illusion of control. Those who have taken such a risk say it was worth it.

3. ACODs Fear Conflict

In years of mediating conflicts and divorces, I never met a person who liked conflict. I've met some who enjoyed a good fight, but even they were rare. Addressing your fear of conflict is not easy. We all have a visceral reaction, commonly called the fight/flight response. For many ACODs, their fear is justified. Conflict was violent in their families.

There are two strategies I suggest for confronting your fear of conflict. The first is to make the environment safe. If you fear the eruption of violence, do not engage a partner in confrontation, or if you must engage, ask a third party to be present. Studies show that most domestic violence occurs in the isolation of the home. Whenever there are friends or extended family present, violence decreases due to the presence of witnesses and help from those who can mediate the situation.

A second strategy is to do the opposite of what most books on conflict counsel. They say, and we have come to believe, that people in conflict should stay in with one another until the conflict is resolved. I disagree. My experience is that people enter conflict with a great lack of clarity and much high feeling. In this state, both parties to the conflict only exacerbate their problems, and the conflict intensifies. I suggest that at the first sign of conflict, both parties separate for a time. During that time, I think it is important to ask yourself these questions: (a) What am I feeling? (b) What is my part in the conflict and where am I responsible? (c) What do I need and want as a resolution?

The reason for this time apart is to be sure you are involved in a real conflict, not in an unrealistic one. In a real conflict, two or more people have a serious disagreement over a substantive issue. In an unrealistic conflict, you may have gotten "triggered" and your reaction is not about the present situation, but about something from your past. In this latter case, do steps a and b above, then meet with the other person to share your findings and acknowledge that you have no conflict. Sometimes both parties to the conflict get triggered and use the fight to avoid doing their own work around their feelings.

In doing the three steps, you clear away material that does not belong in your negotiation. Then you can come together, having taken responsibility for your feelings and your past, and discuss the substantive issues where you are in disagreement.

Here is an example of a couple, both ACODs, who went through an unrealistic conflict and a realistic conflict in the same evening. Jeremy and Kathy were driving to a resort conference center where Kathy had a business meeting. They were looking forward to some time away, and Jeremy was especially interested in playing golf while Kathy attended meetings. Prior to driving to the center, Jeremy had spent time with his father, a man Jeremy rarely saw since his parents' divorce when Jeremy was ten.

As they drove, Kathy suggested they stop for dinner. Jeremy immediately felt irritated. He became critical and cynical at every option Kathy offered. Before long Kathy felt her anger rising. She was ready to blurt out, "Since nothing seems to please you, why don't you pick a place." However, she caught herself and instead said, "Why do you have so much intensity around where we eat? Is it really that important to you? I feel silly fighting over a restaurant. It isn't a big deal to me." At this point Jeremy became silent (which is not the same as withdrawing). He went inside himself and asked, "What am I feeling?" Surprisingly, he immediately got in touch with something that had nothing to do with him and Kathy and a restaurant. He felt deep sadness and loneliness that he didn't know his father. Their meeting had felt superficial, and Jeremy was disappointed that the relationship he wanted with his father simply wasn't there.

The second realization Jeremy had was that it was easier to pick a fight with Kathy than to feel his sadness over his father. The fight actually prevented Jeremy from doing an essential piece of his ACOD recovery that entailed seeing his parents for who they are, not as he has fantasized them.

As soon as Jeremy saw what he was doing, he acknowledged to Kathy that his irritability was not about the choice of restaurant. He shared with her his insight about his father. Kathy and Jeremy did not have a conflict. They easily found a restaurant at the next exit and had a meal that was vastly more enjoyable than if they had dined in the midst of their fight!

Later that evening Jeremy and Kathy had a real conflict over a substantive issue—Kathy's job. Jeremy wanted Kathy to quit her job. He reasoned that his income was enough to support the family, and he wanted Kathy home with their three young children. Jeremy had an aversion to day care. Kathy loved her job, felt stimulated by it, and she believed day care was good for the children. When Kathy and Jeremy went inside themselves to see what they were really feeling, Jeremy got in touch with old feelings about being abandoned as a child during his parents' divorce. Kathy felt fear of financial dependence on Jeremy. She remembered her own mother, who was without any marketable skills at the time of the divorce, and the family's subsequent financial hardships. Kathy also felt she had gifts for business that she wanted to use.

Then Jeremy and Kathy considered the second conflict resolution step: What is my part in the conflict, where am I responsible? They saw that they both had rigid expectations about marriage and family life that they laid on each other. These came from their ACOD experiences and had been unacknowledged in their marriage. Both had decided their family would be the opposite of their families of origin. The problem was that they had not shared these expectations with each other. Just sharing these differences was a relief.

Finally Jeremy and Kathy moved on to answer the third question: What do we each need and want in the situation?

They were able to agree that they wanted a fulfilling life where each one of them would grow. With this agreement Jeremy could see that Kathy needed a job not just for financial security but also for her sense of self. Although Kathy disagreed that day care was bad for the kids, she could see Jeremy's fear. She also missed time with the kids and wished they did more as a family. Out of this desire for more time as a family, Jeremy and Kathy agreed to explore arranging their work schedules in such a way that day care time was cut down. They also coordinated time off from work so the whole family could be together.

Jeremy and Kathy are an ACOD couple who have realized that conflict is a normal part of life together. They are getting much more practical at working through the conflicts using the three steps as each conflict arises. Naturally, the prospect of conflict is still scary. "My gut always wrenches," Kathy said, "but I know I'm not going to die if I ask for what I want. And when we can't agree, we wait with our disagreement until we do get clear."

For some ACODs, conflict was so terrifying that even the prospect of a mild disagreement is paralyzing. They miss chances for intimacy when they flee any hint of conflict. In these instances, I think it is important to say to yourself and to your partner, "I'm really scared of conflict." Saying this out loud helps. Also, it helps to know that your strong reaction is a sign that you have further work to do around the fear you felt from childhood. As you address those old issues, you do feel safer, and conflict is not as unsettling as before.

4. ACODs Take Sides

ACODs have various processes for dealing with the tendency to take sides. One man who admitted he was in early recovery around his ACOD issues says that he makes it a matter of principle not to join any side. He feels at this time in his healing, he is so seduced by belonging to some side that he loses himself completely in the process of "joining up."

Other ACODs have found that when they deal with their issues of belonging, needing a place, and excessive caretaking of others, their "taking sides" behavior greatly diminishes.

Taking sides throws you into the process of dualism. You simplify your world into two choices, black and white. Then you gravitate back and forth between your two choices, with the illusion that one side or the other contains the truth, and therefore security. This is indeed an illusion, however, and some ACODs have had their worlds shattered when they discovered that the story they told themselves about one of their parents' "rightness" in the divorce process proved to be a myth of their own making.

Malcolm struck me as a man whose side-taking behavior had even influenced his choice of career. Malcolm's mother divorced his father when Malcolm was eight. Malcolm lived with his mother and a new stepfather and had infrequent contact with his father, who was a drifter. Malcolm maintained an intense loyalty to his father, which was rarely reciprocated. "I just couldn't bear to see him for the failure that he was. I was desperate for a father I could be proud of, so I defended him and blamed my mother, even though my mother was the one who really hung in there with me." Malcolm went on to a career in law and was attracted to defending powerless, down-and-out people. "I had an intensity about my defense work which was awesome. Unfortunately, I also had the tendency to overlook some of my clients' true defects. Getting them off the hook was my job, not seeing them for who they were." As Malcolm began his recovery around his ACOD issues, his job became more intolerable. "I couldn't blindly defend people who I knew were guilty. I lost my energy and interest in that kind of work. How could I become truthful at one level of my life regarding my father and not be truthful at another level with my basic work?"

Taking sides is a thinking process in a dualistically oriented society where it is believed that things can be simplified into right and wrong. There is much judgmentalism underlying this process: You are good or bad, depending upon those with whom you align. Surprisingly, in recovery you find that the issues are not right, wrong, good, or bad. As adults, we need to seek the truth of our situation, even if the truth means saying, "Oops, I'm wrong." If you value honesty above winning, sides become irrelevant. I believe that even in early recovery, you can come to realize that when you are presented with a situation that requires you to take sides, it is a trap. You must avoid it. For ACODs, it is important always to go back into the self and to stay with your own process. You need to avoid external pulls to take one side or another. It may give you a temporary sense of belonging to join a side, but you run the risk of losing yourself. You must listen carefully to what is true for you.

5. ACODs Feel Abandoned

In fact, ACODs often were abandoned. The two ways in which ACODs felt most abandoned were that they were left physically and emotionally by their parents, and then they left themselves as they stifled their emotions.

You can first stop abandoning yourself. This means that you will have to start focusing on your needs, taking time to nurture yourself, and actually spending time with yourself. This is a singularly new idea for people who leave themselves a lot! Concretely, this means that you will actually do things that are nurturing. You will acknowledge that you are worth something. In this way, you accept responsibility for yourself. A woman ACOD whose job frequently takes her away from home makes it a practice to give herself one day off after each trip, no matter how pressing a schedule she faces. "It would be so easy for me to lose myself in my work. I take the time to read, shop, have a quiet cup of tea. I just give myself time. Otherwise, I begin to feel crazy and abandoned, but no one has left me. I've just left myself." This woman has found a way to handle one of the more seductive ways that ACODs leave themselves. It always seems so very important to respond to the pressures of a busy schedule with more work. It makes leaving yourself seem legitimate. I find that in early recovery, you may need to do less so that you have more time for self-care.

In addition to cutting back on activities, you can be aware of those times when you leave yourself emotionally. Those are the times you feel dead inside. You find yourself without internal emotional responses. Again, these times are good clues that there is something you need to work on, from the present or the past, and the characteristic ACOD response is to "leave" rather than to take care of your needs. You get more astute about your inner process by giving that process time.

You can learn to take time for solitude. This is an important process because, before recovery, ACODs believe that to be alone is to be abandoned. You need to learn the difference between abandonment and solitude. Being alone is wonderful when you spend time with yourself if you are present to the experience; but if you are not present, then you feel abandoned. Many ACODs establish a period every day when they go to a private place, a room or a place in nature, just to be alone and to think, meditate, and let feelings surface. By taking time alone, you get to know yourself and find that you are worth the effort. Although the adults in your life may have left you, you can learn to stay with yourself.

6. ACODs Have Difficulty Setting Limits and Personal Boundaries

Personal boundaries are important. ACODs need to consider the ways they let other people invade them, and the ways they invade others. With others, it is necessary for you to know the minute you feel ill at ease in an interaction. You should pay attention to this awareness and ask yourself how you are feeling unsafe or uncomfortable. Is it because you are losing yourself in relation to the other person? You might ask yourself what you need in this interaction. When facing requests from others, many recovering ACODs say no, or ask for time to consider the request further because they feel overwhelmed in the moment. It is all right not to have a ready answer to every request.

An ACOD who is a lecturer and consultant was enthusiastically approached by a man after one of his speeches. He asked the speaker to consult with his company. Overtaken by the compliment and the sense of affirmation it gave him, the consultant agreed, without checking in with himself. The situation was a disaster from the start. He found himself in over his head with a group that was very troubled. Too late, he realized that had he not let himself be so swayed by praise, he would have assessed the situation more realistically.

From this experience, this ACOD learned not to commit

himself until he gathered more information. Like this man, you can state your needs, gather data, and ask for time before you make a commitment. This process is effective in your personal and professional life.

When you do not respect your own need for boundaries, you rarely respect others' boundaries. If you think you are the one invading others' boundaries, you can get information on the effect you have on others by asking them how they feel around you. In intimate relationships, you can work on your boundary issues by asking your partner to give you feedback when you are overbearing, and you can take the risk to tell him or her when you feel that your limits have been violated.

As your healing of your ACOD issues progresses, you will find that the boundary issue changes. Early on, you may need to keep others very far away just to get space enough to know your own needs. During these times, any attempt by another to come closer to you may feel intrusive. As you become stronger, these same overtures may not feel oppressive at all. You need to give yourself the time to do what feels right in terms of boundaries, for you are building a self in this process, and knowing your limits is an essential aspect of your recovery. It helps to know who you are. Ultimately, you must see that you are the one responsible for setting and maintaining boundaries. You cannot be taken over by another without your letting it happen.

7. ACODs Feel Helpless

As an ACOD, your helplessness manifests itself in three ways: (1) you do not know how to respond to various situations, (2) you stand by, watching, in situations where you should act, and (3) you lack some basic communication and social skills. Sometimes your deficiencies in communication skills contribute to your feeling helpless in the first two situations.

Recovery from this characteristic is greatly facilitated by a mentor or sponsor, someone who is not caught up in the web of helplessness, and who is willing to guide and advise you. Here is an example of how one ACOD made good use of a mentor.

Rich came from a family in which a severely dysfunctional predivorce process lasted seven years, spanning Rich's formative years (six to thirteen). During most of this period, Rich tried to become invisible so as not to add to the burden of divorce. Rich's parents were so enmeshed in their struggles that they neglected parenting their children.

As Rich matured, he found that he had innate gifts for marketing and selling, but he lacked skills for presenting himself and his ideas to coworkers and clients. He also exaggerated small conflicts and withdrew at the slightest hint of trouble. Overall, he was socially immature.

Rich knew he needed to learn some rudimentary skills for relating professionally and personally, so he set about looking for a mentor. He found a man several years older who was a manager in another department. At first Rich just observed this man to see what he could learn from him. He actively watched his mentor, meaning that Rich noted the things his mentor did that were effective. Sometimes Rich wrote down what he learned from interactions with his mentor. These observations confirmed for Rich that he had chosen a worthy mentor for he saw him as a person he admired—one who was good in business and one who had integrity in dealing with others.

Next Rich requested a meeting with his mentor. Rich determined to be honest with this man, and so he simply shared with the manager his desire to be more effective in selling and his awareness that he didn't have all the skills he needed. Rich also gave the manager some family background to explain why he was inept socially. Finally, Rich said that he knew he needed help in several areas, that he admired the manager, and that he hoped the manager would be willing to assist him. The manager was impressed with Rich's honesty and his willingness to seek help. He felt complimented that Rich sought his advice. He agreed to meet periodically with Rich to coach Rich on his presentations to clients, and he also offered to give Rich feedback about his interactions with coworkers. He also invited Rich to meetings that he believed would enable Rich to see other effective selling styles. Rich maintained a productive and satisfying relationship with his mentor for many years. He was to say of the relationship that it wasn't a father-son relationship and it wasn't a political power relationship, although it could easily have become either or both. Instead it was two humans who cared about each other and who grew in mutual respect. Rich subsequently became an outstanding salesman, the recipient of many awards. Today he congratulates himself for having the courage to ask for help, and he congratulates his mentor for superb modeling.

Good mentors and good sponsors will support you in your recovery process. They will not tell you what to do, and this is vital to your recovery. In overcoming helplessness, it is important that you do not just turn your life over to someone else and blindly follow their advice. That would be another form of helplessness. You need to make your own decisions. Others may assist you by giving you information and the benefit of their experience, but you have to do it yourself.

Like Rich you can watch others and learn from them how to take more initiative. This is where participating in a support group can be so valuable. You see models of behavior and stories of success. You can see what works and what does not, and find a style that is comfortable for you.

8. ACODs Have Excessive Needs for a Home and Economic Security

This is a characteristic you really need to grapple with because the consequences are disastrous when you react blindly out of your ACOD history. Many ACODs told me stories of taking jobs they hated or marrying people they did not really love, just to escape the fear of economic insecurity. Your behavior around these issues is often reactive rather than truly self-nurturing. You know what you don't want, but you don't know what you do want.

A woman ACOD shared her story with me, one that is common among ACODs. She said, "After my parents' divorce, which occurred when I was fourteen, I went through typical teen stuff but with more intensity, I suppose. I did drugs and I was never without a boyfriend. I was in a lot of pain and I did some crazy stuff to numb my pain. I hated my new stepfather, and as soon as I could, I married and got away from home. I see now that I hooked up with the first man who came along who seemed to offer me a way out. This marriage was a disaster. I'm sure you're not surprised that I married someone just like my father. He was having affairs within eighteen months of our wedding. So much for marrying for love, or my illusion of love. In my next marriage I determined I needed a responsible man who could hold a job. I got that and a lot of abuse as well. I finally learned the hard way that each of my important life choices has been reactive, and they have not resulted in the security I long for."

So many ACODs identify with the above story. The search for home and economic security is important, but it should not be an end in itself. These things are the result of your recovery, not the starting point of recovery. As you begin your personal work around acknowledging your ACOD characteristics and healing from them, you become more solid in yourself. You begin to have your own preferences, your own style, and your own sense of priorities about what you need economically. This is what it means to "come home to yourself" and to find that you must first be "at home" with yourself. Your external environment is a mirror of your internal environment. As you claim your identity and acknowledge your needs, you will be surprised how quickly issues with money and home solve themselves. Keep in mind the title of the popular book by Marsha Sinetar: *Do What You Love, the Money Will Follow*. In the case of ACODs this is especially apt, but I would nuance it differently: Do your ACOD recovery and a home and economic security will follow.

9. ACODs Idealize and Blame Their Parents and Other Authority Figures

I rarely meet an ACOD who is not working on some aspect of his or her relationship with one or both parents. A common step, and one that is essential for recovery in this area, is breaking down the illusions you have created about your parents. So often, you idealized one or the other parent, creating incredible stories about why they divorced. Your illusion-making was often directed toward the parent with whom you spent less time, or whom you pitied.

A young man, now in his twenties, chose to believe for years that his father had been terribly wronged by his mother, who had initiated the divorce. He saw his father regularly and experienced several incidents where his father was drunk, violent, and irresponsible with the children. Still, in the son's eyes, the father could do no wrong, and the mother was seen as the cause of the divorce. She was the one who denied him a chance to be with his father. The illusion crumbled when the son entered treatment for his drug addiction. During family week, his father acknowledged his part in the dysfunctional family, and that he, too, had a substance addiction that had ruined his life. For the first time, the son let himself see that perhaps his mother had grounds for her action.

Not many of us receive the gift of a parent who is willing to take an active role in breaking down one's illusions about them. Most ACODs have to work on this process alone, and there are steps you can take. ACODs have several ways of seeing their parents more truthfully. One way is by seeking information from relatives and siblings about their perception of the parent. This can be tricky because sometimes relatives have their own unresolved issues that they project on the parent. Sharing perceptions with siblings is often useful in breaking your illusions. Frequently brothers and sisters have vastly different experiences of the same parent. Sharing information with them can be a reality check and it can also move you to broaden your view of a parent.

Where possible, it is important to speak with your parents and ask them about the divorce and what they were feeling, how it was for them. Because denial pervades the dysfunctional divorce, you may find gaining a clear perspective on your parents is difficult. Trust yourself and be open to new information. You may never get the whole truth, and you will have to see what is true for you. Ultimately, you need to come to your own understanding of your parents and the divorce, but it needs to be an understanding based on the truth, as much as you can know it, and not some fantasy you create so you feel good.

Often these truths are surprises, and they can be painful awakenings. Your parents are not the people you fabricated. Essential to your healing is forgiving yourself for creating the illusions in the first place and forgiving your parents for the ways they may have harmed you. This process is called making amends, and it is important to do it in order to heal yourself and to reestablish bonds with parents and others.

This process of dismantling your illusions and making amends is a first step in dealing with the confusion that surrounds your parents. Seeing yourself for who you are, and your parents for who they are, facilitates all subsequent processes and enables you to get on with resolving your other issues with your parents, issues of anger and disappointment about what your parents did. These are old feelings you need to work through, and you can do so with individual and group support.

10. ACODs Have Unrealistic Expectations for Their Relationships and Marriages

This area is central because ACODs tend to focus their unresolved issues onto their relationships. So much of your healing has a direct impact on your relationships. And even at a societal level, our healing in the area of relationships can ensure that dysfunctional family patterns are not perpetuated in future generations. Unfortunately, you get almost no help from society in understanding the healthy relationship. The media provide you with plenty of examples of how not to do relationships, but models for healthy relationships are scarce.

ACODs who are actively working on this area approach their recovery in a variety of ways. Some go to marriage counselors for help with communication skills. Others use books to help them understand and articulate better the feelings in their relationships. Many attend Sex, Love, and Relationship Addicts Anonymous (SLAA), finding support there for moving out of addictive behaviors.

It is essential to break out of preconceived ideas about what a relationship should be. You have almost as many illusions about relationships and marriage as you do about your parents.

Whenever you are in a reactive stance, you know you are in trouble. When your relationships have to be the opposite of your parents', you are setting yourself up for failure because you are still using them as your measure. In a very real way, their divorce still rules your choices.

An ACOD woman spoke wisely about this when she said, "I am going step-by-step with my own marriage, in the moment. When issues arise, I meet them, and my husband and I are evolving our relationship rather than fitting the relationship into a preconceived idea. It is scary, fun, and we never know what is next, but we are feeling fully alive and that is wonderful."

Having expectations for your relationships is burdensome because you take yourself out of the process described above, and you begin to control for certain outcomes. You need to distinguish between having expectations and communicating needs. They are different. When you communicate your needs, you take responsibility for yourself in the relationship. You may or may not get what you want, and you must deal with the pain generated by that. With expectations, you establish certain needs as absolute and set those "out there." When the other does not conform, you use the expectation to judge the person and judge the rightness or wrongness of the relationship.

An ACOD couple exemplify the difference between having expectations and communicating needs. Mark and Janet were going to take their first vacation in several years. They decided on a week in Bermuda. They both had expectations for the time in Bermuda and of each other. Janet wanted to explore beaches, get some exercise, and learn to scuba dive. She had several issues she wanted to discuss with Mark, issues they never seemed to have time for at home. She wanted to discuss concerns she was feeling about their six-year-old son, she wanted to share her new thoughts about her art, and she hoped they would have long, luxurious hours in bed together. Actually she envisioned paradise and had been fantasizing about it for weeks. Mark, on the other hand, was exhausted from work. He wanted to sleep until he felt caught up on rest, read on the beach, and have all meals brought to him. He wanted to get away from stress and that meant all stress—work and family. His attitude was, "Don't bother me. I need time off."

Janet and Mark traveled to Bermuda with their own separate expectations quietly nursed and never expressed, except in little ways like, "I can hardly wait to hit the beach with a book" (Mark), and "I've got so much to tell you" (Janet). Their expectations collided in Bermuda. By the third day of vacation, Janet felt abandoned ("Mark won't do anything with me"). Mark felt hassled ("She won't leave me alone. I'm desperate for space and time to zone out"). Both had made their expectations a rigid requirement for having a good time, and they held on to the expectations as if they were a sacred right. The issue became, "How do I control you to get what I need?" They entered into bargaining to get some of their needs met. "I'll go for a walk on the beach with you if you'll let me read." Midway into the vacation they were miserable and totally exhausted with controlling one another.

This experience is in contrast with simply communicating your needs. In that process, Janet and Mark could simply have said, "Here is what I want to do on vacation." Janet could have invited Mark to join her in her jaunts. Mark could have taken time to see if he really wanted to join Janet. If he didn't, he should have said so. It is then up to Janet to deal with her feelings around his refusal. Too often ACODs interpret others' refusals of their invitations as rejections of them. They personalize. It is not necessarily true that Mark doesn't want to spend time with Janet. He wants to spend time with himself. Against the background of her expectation she interprets his refusal as a rejection of her when in reality it has nothing to do with her.

Sometimes when you communicate your needs, you get exactly what you ask for. Sometimes you don't. When you don't, you have an opportunity to feel the feelings that arise for you. That is not the end of the world, it is just a normal process. And it is a gift. For when you don't get what you want, you have the opportunity to learn to let go—a process that was difficult for you as a child and that you need to learn as an adult.

All relationships and marriage choices are dependent upon doing your personal work first. Too often you believe a relationship will solve your problems. The truth is that you are the problem. Until you heal individually, you bring all your ACOD issues right into the relationship. You do not have to be rigid, believing that until you become the perfect person you can't be in a relationship, but too many ACODs have entered relationships long before they were ready, then expected that their partner would do for them what they would not do for themselves. First, you need to attend to yourself. Then you need to trust the process of the relationship, and finally, you need to stay committed to doing your personal work all the days of your life.

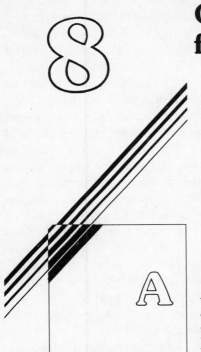

Other Resources for Healing

t no other time in history have there been as many resources for healing from the trauma of divorce as now exist. Fifteen million Americans meet in self-help groups every day to discuss their issues and to recover through peer sharing and programs of mutual support. Although ACOD characteristics are only now being identified, I believe there are sources for help available, and I recommend seeking some sort of help in facing ACOD issues. ACODs already feel isolated with the burden of their experiences. Why tough it out alone when so many heal successfully with the support of others?

Counseling/Therapy

ACODs have sought various kinds of therapy, with mixed results. Since addiction is an issue with many ACODs, they are well advised to avoid psychiatrists and psychologists who rely heavily on medication as their main method of dealing with

143

feelings. ACODs with addictions who have gone this route report years wasted in expensive therapy, only to have to recover from addiction to whatever medication was prescribed. Their feelings remained to be dealt with after they terminated with these professionals.

Recently, at a conference, a woman asked me if I believed that therapists who had not experienced abuse could understand and help ACODs who had abuse in their backgrounds. Her question interested me because I believe at one time in my life I would readily have asserted that therapists who had experienced the same issues as the client were more effective. I now believe that shared experience is not the main criterion for effective therapy. More important is whether the therapist will facilitate the client in working through his or her issues without getting in the way or subtly controlling that person. The "helping" needs to give way to facilitating the process of the client so that clients experience their own power to heal themselves.

This is a key area for ACODs. They already feel helpless and abandoned, so to seek solutions from the outside results in their not developing their inner strength. Therapists with answers, insights, interpretations, and ideas may be stimulating and interesting, but they rarely facilitate ACOD recovery.

I believe that many therapists have unresolved issues of their own around divorce, and it is sometimes difficult for them to avoid giving advice to their ACOD clients. I recently observed a therapist work with an ACOD couple who were struggling with their relationship and considering separating from each other. Rather than helping them explore such an option, the therapist rhapsodized about how deep and profound their spiritual bond was to one another, so profound that one often knew what the other was thinking before it was expressed. I considered these comments by the therapist to be a subtle form of manipulation. I watched the confusion on the couple's faces as they tried to seek an appropriate solution for their present troubles while the therapist romanticized about one aspect of their relationship. The therapist was not so blatant as to say, "I think you two should stay together." He just made their relationship seem more ideal than it was.

Several ACODs attributed their healing to facilitators—

therapists who stayed with them and created a safe environment, but who did not get in the way of the ACOD's own inner process. From this, these ACODs learned that reaching out for help did not mean they lost themselves in the helper, but that they could truly do their own personal work in the presence of someone who "waited with" them. I believe this style of therapy or facilitating is preferable, and ACODs should not be shy about shopping around until they find a person they believe can be with them as they go through their own process of healing.

Varieties of Group Support

I believe self-help groups are effective environments for ACOD recovery.These groups address the problems of isolation by providing a setting in which the ACOD hears others who have had similar experiences. The opportunities to hear others' stories helps you remember your own pain, which you may have repressed for years. You also see examples of those who are further along in their healing than you are.

For ACODs who are struggling with addiction and/or incest and physical-abuse issues, there are established groups that are based on the model first pioneered by Alcoholics Anonymous. Commonly called Twelve Step programs, these programs exist in most cities, are free, and are open to anyone with a sincere desire to stop practicing his or her particular addiction. (Although incest is not an addiction, a Twelve Step—based program is still beneficial because it reduces isolation, furthers knowledge through information, and provides support. In fact, there are Incest Survivors Anonymous groups in many cities.) Because our addictions and our physical-abuse issues are so central, it is necessary to confront them directly. Your ACOD recovery cannot go forward if you are numbing yourself with an addiction.

Later I'll discuss ACOD recovery groups based on the Twelve Step model. If, however, you are not ready to begin with an ACOD recovery group, you can still benefit from attendance at any one of a variety of existing Twelve Step groups. The most well-known are Alcoholics Anonymous and Al-Anon. There are also Adult Children of Addictive and Dysfunctional Family groups and Codependents Anonymous groups, all of which ACODs have found helpful.

Should you attend a Twelve Step group if ACOD issues are your main focus? Yes. In the absence of an ACOD group, I recommend attendance at some Twelve Step group even if its focus is not your particular problem. As I describe below, Twelve Step groups help you confront some of your generic ACOD issues such as helplessness, abandonment, control, and relationship problems. Rather than being just an antidote for a particular addiction, they show you another paradigm for solving your problems and living your life. If you are concerned that your ACOD recovery is blocked because you are abusing substances or you are addicted to romance, sex, relationships, spending, working, etc., all the more reason to confront the addiction in a Twelve Step program. Lastly, you may be confused about what you need. Consider attending some Twelve Step meetings to explore whether there is anything you can learn. You may find you do need to be there or you may not. It is up to you.

Why do Twelve Step recovery groups work for ACODs? They work because they build in processes that directly confront the dysfunctional behaviors you learned in your divorcing family:

• *You feel shame so you isolate and try to do it yourself.* The Twelve Step program functions as a group, so it is hard to hide and remain in isolation. There are others like you so it helps you look at yourself.

• *You feel judgmental about your past and your divorcing parents.* You feel critical about the mistakes you believe your parents made. Twelve Step recovery counsels you to stay with your issues, not with someone else's.

• *You feel helpless to do anything in your life.* The Twelve Steps are a definite program of action. You can work the steps of the program, which is a way to address your helplessness.

• *You feel abandoned and you leave yourself.* Twelve Step groups have sponsors available. These are men and women who are further along in their recovery from their particular addiction than you are, and who are available to you to help you work your recovery program. You are not alone. A good sponsor does not necessarily have to be an ACOD. Their value to you is that they know how the Twelve Step program works. They guide you through it. You make your own application to your issues.

• *You have become overly responsible for others.* Twelve Step recovery admonishes you to do your own program and let others do theirs. By learning to respect yourself you respect others.

• *You try to control your relationships, and what others think and feel.* Twelve Steps groups have two guidelines that help you here. There is no cross talk in meetings, which means you stay with your own reactions. You don't busy yourself discussing with others during the meetings. In addition, you don't give advice in Twelve Step meetings. You speak from your experience, using "I" statements. This keeps you focused on why you are at the meeting, to do your program and not someone else's.

• *You fear conflict and take sides.* In Twelve Step groups, there is the deliberate avoidance of politics, religion, and divisive topics. The purpose of the group is the recovery of each member, not positions on outside issues.

• *You have difficulties with intimate relationships.* Twelve Step recovery groups give you one model for healthy relating. You see and hear others sharing their stories, but not advising you on yours. You hear others speaking honestly about where they are today, without judgmentalism. You experience acceptance of yourself with all your defects, and support for your recovery, no matter how long it takes. Rather than overwhelming others with your knowledge, your power comes from disclosing yourself and giving of yourself. All of these processes are in contrast to your divorcing family, where feelings were strongly negative and were usually dumped inappropriately on you.

As an ACOD you suffered the loss of your ability to be just yourself in your family's divorce. In the Twelve Step group you are supported in being yourself.

ACOD Recovery Groups

Taking a cue from the enormous success of Twelve Step groups around the nation, I believe that ACODs would do well to form ACOD recovery groups. How would you go about setting up such a group and how would an ACOD recovery group function? Here are a few ideas.

1. Setting Up an ACOD Recovery Group

Advertise the formation of an ACOD recovery group in your local newspaper. Many newspapers have self-help sections where other Twelve Step groups are listed. Some people have notices on community bulletin boards and in service agencies and hospitals. The notice could read: "Adult children of divorce group meeting at (location and time). This group is open to all adults who suffer from the experience of their parents' divorce and who wish to heal through sharing their experience, hope, and strength. Meetings are free and confidential." It is usually a good idea to list a first name and a phone number where people can get more information.

2. The Format of an ACOD Recovery Group

In the first meeting of the ACOD group it will be necessary to agree on the format of the meeting and the ground rules. I offer the following suggestions about the meeting because these guidelines have worked well in fifty years of Twelve Step-based self-help groups.

- Leadership. Someone needs to open and close the meeting. Leaders ought to rotate from meeting to meeting so that one person isn't always doing it. By rotating leadership all members of the group take responsibility for the group process.
- Introduction. The leader should open the meeting and welcome everyone. Such a welcome could be like this: "Hello, everyone. My name is _____ and I am an adult child of divorce. This is the

weekly meeting of ACODs of [state the location]. Before we introduce ourselves I'd like to read the purpose of our group."

The leader or someone the leader selects then reads the group purpose:

"The purpose of ACOD recovery groups is to heal from the long-term effects of divorce that we experienced as children and that are still with us. We acknowledge that we were powerless over our parents' decision to divorce. We seek through this group to know and acknowledge the truth inherent in our own stories, to honestly share our experience with other ACODs, and to heal our lives and our relationships through mutual support of one another."

• The leader then asks the group members to introduce themselves by first name only. Use of first names ensures anonymity. Group members may wish to identify their age at the time of the divorce, although in many groups that may not be necessary.

• Next the leader describes the ground rules of the meeting. Some tried-and-true ground rules are:

—Use of first names only.

—Confidentiality. What is said in the meeting remains in the meeting. This provides safety so that members can be completely honest and not fear repercussions or judgment.

—No cross talk. This means that you are not in the meeting to advise, therapize, agree, or disagree with the other members of the group. You are there to share what you need to share and to listen to others. The ACOD group is not a discussion group where all the members have to leave the meeting of one mind. After a person shares, it is not advisable to respond to that person. Instead, go on to the next person. You may disagree with some of the things you hear. You can take in those things that make sense to you and you can leave the rest. This process is part of your learning to set appropriate boundaries. When you busy yourself advising other people in the meeting, you cease focusing on yourself and you once again leave your own process. This is your time; other people can take care of themselves.

—No pressure. There should be no pressure on anyone to share his/her experience or story. Some may spend many meetings just listening and learning. It is okay to pass. Those who do choose to speak should not monopolize the meeting. It is sometimes necessary for the leader to ask a group member to be brief so that others have a chance to speak.

—Time. You should establish the beginning and ending time of the meeting and then stick to it. If the meeting has no boundaries in terms of time, group members feel trapped. It is easier to attend an ACOD meeting faithfully when you know its length than if it just rambles on. Sixty to ninety minutes is the usual time for meetings. It is the leader's responsibility to call an end to the meeting.

—Many Twelve Step meetings end with the Serenity Prayer. I think it is an appropriate way to close an ACOD meeting. It reads: "God, grant me the serenity to accept the things I cannot change, the courage to change the things I can, and the wisdom to know the difference."

Now you have the format of the meeting. But what are you going to do in these meetings? There are several approaches. One approach is to ask one or two group members to share their ACOD story, telling about how the divorce affected them and how they are working on their issues today. After their talk, other group members may want to share those memories that are sparked in them as a result of hearing the speakers.

Another approach is to work each of the ten ACOD characteristics over a series of ten meetings. Someone could read a paragraph or two about the characteristic. Then the meeting would be open to people sharing how they experienced the characteristic as children or adults.

A third approach is for the group members to brainstorm a list of topics and agree to use those topics in subsequent meetings. At first the group may be so new that it is good to have ten ACOD characteristics to structure the meetings around. However, as the group goes deeper into their ACOD issues, I believe there will be no dearth of material.

ACOD Life Inventory

Are there other tools you can use to become more aware of your issues as an ACOD? Again, taking our cue from Twelve Step groups, you can write your ACOD life inventory. This is a process that aids you in remembering, and remembering is often difficult for ACODs. The life inventory enables you to assess the effects of ACOD experiences and characteristics, as well as to get a clearer picture of yourself.

There is a simple way of going about the ACOD inventory. First you must set aside time to actually work on the inventory. Doing it on the way to work in the morning isn't the right place or time. Set aside some quiet time and a place where you won't be disturbed. Then remember back as far as you can to the first time you recall being aware of the distress in your family related to divorce. In the beginning you may have only one or two memories. This is okay. More memories will come as you are ready for them.

Beginning with your earliest memories, list:

1. *What was happening in my family?* Make this a nonjudgmental description and make it as detailed as you can. Here is one description written by a twenty-four-year-old ACOD: "I am in my bed. I am six years old. Mom is sitting on the edge of my bed. She is crying and telling me that she and Dad are getting a divorce. She tells me that I did not have to feel responsible for what they are doing. She says she loves me and that she will not leave me. Outside it is raining."
2. *Describe how you felt.* It is all right just to list the feelings without explanation, e.g., frightened, lonely, scared, anxious, worried, etc.
3. *Write how you reacted, what you did.* Our twenty-four-year-old above wrote: "I curled under my covers and cried myself to sleep. The next day I

went to school and I told my teacher my mom and dad were getting a divorce. She hugged me but I still felt scared and lonely."

4. *What are you feeling as an adult?* In this part of the inventory, the ACOD looks at current issues. Continuing with the example, the young man writes: "I feel unsure of myself, especially in relationships where I get close to people. I still am scared of being left, so I don't let people get too close."

The inventory process can aid you in becoming more explicit in acknowledging the truth of your story. Also, inevitably, new memories are jogged as you do your inventory.

Another approach to the ACOD inventory is to use the ten ACOD characteristics and to list when you first began to notice these characteristics in yourself. A description of how you manifest the particular characteristic, and how you feel about it, rounds out this inventory.

As you take your ACOD inventory, it is likely that you will begin to feel things that were buried. You may uncover incest memories or have realizations that are especially troubling. I believe inventories are powerful processes and should not be done in isolation. You should seek a sponsor or other ACODs who can support you in this process. You can turn to them or to a trusted friend when you feel overwhelmed.

The Power of ACOD Recovery

"Is recovery possible, is it worth it?" asked a woman at a conference where I was describing ACOD characteristics. She acknowledged that she identified many of the characteristics in her own life, yet she felt so overwhelmed that she wanted to avoid doing anything. "I want to crawl in a hole and wait for it to go away," she confessed.

I believe this woman's reaction is typical and normal. On first hearing or reading about the characteristics, they seem overwhelming. The problem with your ACOD past is that it does not go away. It is somewhat like a physical illness, in which the symptoms intensify and then gradually, with treatment, you get better. If you do nothing, however, the ACOD "disease" does not heal on its own. Those who are most acutely aware of this fact are people who find themselves replicating their dysfunctional family's behavior in their own families and seeing the effects. Their children become mirrors of themselves.

Eileen, a fifty-year-old ACOD, said she had to learn the hard way about her control and perfectionism, two characteristics she had developed in her divorcing family. After her parents' divorce, Eileen lived with her mother, but she longed for her father's approval. She felt she could make up to him for the pain of the divorce by excelling at school. Her father did nothing to discourage her efforts, and in fact, he was pleased that Eileen was so similar to himself, a perfectionist workaholic. Although Eileen did not live with him, he felt she was turning out to be more like him than her mother. He took this development to be a victory. (It is amazing the way divorcing spouses can keep the battle going long after the war is declared over.)

As an adult, Eileen went through two marriages. In each, her control, perfectionism, and excessive working drove her spouses away. It was during her third marriage that Eileen hit bottom with these issues. She was beginning to face her issues inherited from her father. It felt as if things were improving when suddenly her twenty-five-year-old daughter died of a heart attack. Eileen's daughter, a recovering alcoholic, switched her addiction from alcohol to work, the addiction of choice for two generations of her family. When she died, she was in school full-time, and working two part-time jobs. Reflecting on her daughter's death, Eileen said, "I couldn't keep my daughter alive. I obviously learned there were things beyond my control. I also learned that my ACOD characteristics, along with my addiction to work, were family patterns. I saw how deadly they can be, if not interrupted. I lost my daughter, and I'm sorry to say it took that to wake me up."

Eileen is an extreme case, and yet I wonder if she is that different from many ACODs. Many ACODs lose their children and loved ones to a slower death than Eileen's daughter's heart attack. They drive them away with their control and aggression. They miss opportunities for intimacy because they fear intimacy, or they set such unrealistic expectations for relationships. ACODs' kids feel unsupported because ACODs become helpless in the face of conflict. Indeed, their loved ones slowly die, emotionally, because ACODs are not available to them when they are immersed in the disease of these ACOD patterns.

I believe recovery from your ACOD past is necessary. ACODs are the best testimony to that. Your parents did not do their personal work. Now you carry their legacy. You need to recover for yourself and for future generations.

Recovery is also possible. Every day I hear another story that convinces me that we are not destined to live out the old patterns. For example, Eileen was beginning to address her dysfunctional controlling behavior before her daughter's death. Since then, she has made changes. For the first time in her life, she began an MBA program because she wanted to, not to please someone else. She says she doesn't care whether she ever graduates. She is doing the program for herself. Eileen is seeing a counselor who is facilitating her as she reconstructs her memories of her childhood, and in seeing her father for who he is. She is attending Workaholics Anonymous meetings because she is addicted to excessive "doing." She says that for the first time in her life, she feels in charge without being controlling. In the past, she had so many unresolved issues from her dysfunctional family, she believed that control was a way to keep the issues at bay. Now she knows that strategy has the opposite effect. The more she controls, the worse things become. Today, she is learning to let go. She meets things as they come. Surprisingly, she feels more alive. Everyone around her is grateful, for she is more relaxed and more available to her loved ones.

Eileen has progressed in her recovery. Others change in smaller ways. A comment I heard many times from those ACODs who completed my questionnaire was, "Just having a name for what I have been feeling is so helpful to me. I feel as if I walked out of a fog."

Two twenty-seven-year-old men discussed the steps they are taking. They admit to being ACODs, and although they are wary of all of the activities that are suggested for recovery, still they are doing some things. One attends a group meeting once a week in which he deals with current issues in his life. He is beginning to see the way his family's dysfunctional patterns caused the divorce. The other says he struggles with being extremely independent. He never lets anyone do anything for him, except his mother. While his independence was an advantage, it also led to isolation. He still has problems with girlfriends, who find him aloof. Recently, he is recognizing how lonely his independence makes him. He is doing some reading on these topics and may join his friend at the weekly group meeting. These are small steps and they are just right for these two young men.

It is difficult to discuss successful ACOD recovery because we are only now naming the phenomenon. However, there are people who are working on these issues, and their stories have common elements. It begins with naming, actually having a label for what you are experiencing. Whether that name is one or all of the ten ACOD characteristics, the important thing is that naming reduces denial. After naming, you gather more information. You read, you discuss with your peers, you check out your perceptions with others. At this point, the recovery is still in your head. It is at the level of insight. Insight is wonderful. It is a relief and it makes sense out of confusing bits of data. Unfortunately, insight itself is not recovery.

After naming, some ACODs stop. You have the information that explains your present behavior. You mistakenly believe that, armed with this information, you will be different. This rarely happens, and you have the frustrating experience of continuing former behavior even though you know better. The next stage occurs when you step out of isolation and put the information you have about yourself into some other arena. You join an ACOD group, go to therapy, begin a Twelve Step program. Sometimes you do all three. In these instances, you seek support from others. You are ready to identify yourself as an ACOD, and you are ready to learn more about yourself, feel your feelings, and become more honest about your dysfunctional family.

A third stage is the realization that ACOD recovery is a lifelong process. It is a paradigm shift away from old dysfunctional behaviors to new, healthy ones. The change occurs at all levels of life. You begin with the microcosm of your own family, past and present. You take responsibility for your own process. As you do that, you begin to trust your process and appreciate its resilience and its inner wisdom. As you let go of old behaviors and attitudes, you let go of assumptions about such basic issues as relationships, intimacy, and family. The possibility that any of these might take on a new form is now seen as an option rather than a threat. You can choose or not choose, as you wish.

You should never underestimate the significance of your ACOD recovery for society. The common wisdom is that we grow strong in the weak places. In our society, the "family" is in deep trouble. Culturally, it is one of our weakest places. Everywhere, families appear to be floundering, yet each ACOD who recovers is a personal, private revolution in the culture of the family. Your recovery teaches us about resilience and hope, giving all of us second and third chances to form relationships that are life giving, not life denying. A profound shift is in the making, and recovering ACODs are helping it happen.

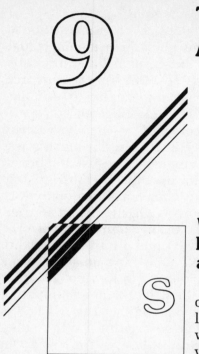

The Good News About Divorce

When Divorce Is a Positive Solution, with a Positive Outcome

So far, I have been describing the long-term effects of divorces in which children developed survival behaviors that proved dysfunctional in adult life. Having seen the pain of many ACODs, it would be tempting to reach the conclusion that divorce is "bad." But after scores of interviews with ACODs, I am still certain that divorce itself is a neutral act. It is the process of divorce that affects children and results in their being problem-afflicted ACODs. Nevertheless, I was heartened by the many ACODs who were quick to point out that divorce had its positive aspects, as well. In fact, in a large number of stories, the divorce was far preferable to staying together through years of dysfunction.

There are degrees of wellness with divorce. In families where fighting and violence prevailed, the divorce was a blessed relief. It provided safety where none had previously existed. It provided limits, when before the divorce the children had felt perilously adrift, as victims. One ACOD looked back on her family's experience with new appreciation for her mother when she said, "I do believe the act of divorcing my alcoholic and irresponsible father was the most responsible action Mother could have taken at the time."

Many ACODs witnessed a parent calling a halt to unacceptable conduct on the part of the other spouse, thus modeling to their children that respect and responsibility are indispensable family virtues. Although no ACOD enjoyed divorce, some acknowledge a basic rightness in the action to terminate a marriage that was painful and hurtful to children.

Several ACODs say they felt cared for by parents who were honest about the fact that their dysfunctional relationship was damaging to their children. A young man whose perfectionist father yelled and screamed at him over the slightest mistake said he learned he wasn't to blame when his father finally took responsibility for his own behavior. ACODs who had an overbearing parent often experienced a respite after the divorce.

ACODs appreciate the courage it took for their parents to admit incompatibility, and to do something about it. They witnessed the suffering of the parent who was not ready or willing to divorce, in contrast to the parent who was initiating the divorce. They are realistic about the fact that what was positive for one spouse was often devastating for the other. ACODs learned early that two apparently opposite views can both be true.

In the positive divorces, there is no denial. All parties own up to what they are feeling and needing. Many ACODs say the divorce resulted in improved communication. For the first time, they heard their parents expressing their true feelings. This, in itself, was a benefit of their divorce. Although painful, the effect of many divorces is that they "woke up" the family. There is no more pretending that everything is okay. A man whose parents divorced when he was thirteen said he finally realized his father was a one-dimensional person who believed "you should screw them before they screw you." This unspoken attitude had pervaded the family. With the divorce, the father's beliefs were in the open and had less power over their lives.

Many ACODs lose contact with one parent after a divorce. In the positive divorces, ACODs remember getting to know a parent better. In the positive divorce, neither parent undermines the other in front of the children. There is a basic respect for the child's relationship with the other parent, and this attitude opens new doors for children. It is not only that ACODs get to know their parents, it is that they see them for who they are. They see beyond their illusions about their parents.

Overall, ACODs believe the decision to divorce was probably correct. When the process was clean and straightforward, and honored each person's feelings, it was not traumatic nor long-term in its consequences. Unfortunately, in only a handful of divorces did the process evolve so well. The usual case was that divorce was difficult, tension filled, and frightening. In these cases, ACODs carry more long-term consequences. But even in these difficult divorces, a number of ACODs feel that the outcome was positive and their situation was better after the divorce.

These ACODs have characteristics that they believe distinguish them as survivors of divorce. These characteristics are the flip side of the dysfunction arising from divorce. They are the strengths emerging from the divorce experience. You can learn to make them your strengths as well.

Characteristics of ACODs for Whom Divorce Was Positive

Independence

Many ACODs found themselves on their own as a result of their parents' divorce. Many times they were denied financial support for higher education, and the divorce lowered their standard of living. They began working at an early age, and they realized they had to take responsibility for themselves.

In divorced families, as the custodial parent (usually the mother) is working and rebuilding a social life, children take on greater responsibility in the household. They learn to cook, clean, and do chores. A woman ACOD puts it this way: "I knew I had to watch out for myself. It wasn't that my mother did not love me. I knew she did. She just had all she could do to keep our home together, and Dad was beginning a new life with a new wife. I felt I had to take care of myself, first, and not expect that my father would always be there for me."

There is another way that these ACODs are independent. They are independent of the feelings of others. They are not so enmeshed in others' troubles. Earlier, we saw that many ACODs have difficulty with relationships, either hanging on to others or pushing them away. This is true, yet ACODs who saw divorce as positive seem to have a healthy sense of themselves as separate from others. They are not isolated from others. They are possessed of a sense of self. They want to make their own decisions and are willing to take the consequences of their mistakes. They do not refuse help when it is offered, and they have developed a sense of self-reliance such that they would not be helpless if others were not available to them.

Resilience

I considered naming this characteristic "toughness," for ACODs sometimes do develop an exterior that hides great vulnerability. Still, I think "resilience" is more appropriate. ACODs, themselves, comment wonderingly about their ability to bounce back. They feel that they witnessed things in their families that were deeply disturbing, yet they find that they go on.

They attribute their resilience to the example of one or both parents, who refused to give up in the face of divorce. ACODs watched mothers who had been withdrawn and without skills go back to school, get jobs, and support a family. They watched fathers learn to parent, when before the divorce they had been inept around the house.

ACODs have an inner strength. A young woman who began a house-painting business to help her get through school said, "I was catapulted into the real world after my folks divorced, and I was scared. Yet, I knew I had some kind of strong core in myself that I could rely on." Indeed, ACODs do feel a certain toughness inside. They are not surprised by much. They feel they have seen a lot, and often at an early age. Joked one ACOD, "Working as an orderly in a mental hospital wasn't at all shocking to me. I had seen it all at home, years before."

Several ACODs are sanguine about their own marriages, saying that they hope they will work out, but if they don't, they know it will not be the end of the world. Knowing it will not mean the end of the world seems to be the hallmark of these ACODs' resilience. They've been there before. They know they can make it. They will learn as they go, and they don't give up.

Access to Feelings

This characteristic, more than any other, distinguishes the positive outcome of divorce from the negative for the ACODs. Scores of ACODs grew up with frozen feelings. It was unsafe to feel in their dysfunctional, divorcing families because there was no one there who could provide safety. Consequently, ACODs reach adulthood completely out of touch with feelings, or they may have only one feeling—anger.

In families where divorce was positive, ACODs had different experiences. They saw their parents expressing feelings, and in many cases the feelings were not directed inappropriately onto the children, but they were not hidden, either. As children, these ACODs were encouraged to feel, and feelings were not judged. They just "were," and they were allowed to run their course. A forty-year-old woman remembers her parents' divorce well. It happened when she was twelve, and she curled up into a tight ball and cried and cried. No one tried to stop her or tell her things would be better. Her tears lasted for days. Occasionally, her father would hold her while she cried, but mainly he was present without being intrusive. She learned to respect her response to situations and to let herself take the time that she needed when she had strong feelings. In adulthood, she usually knows what she feels about something almost immediately. She is in contrast to those ACODs who, weeks after an event, finally have a reaction to it, and then they aren't sure if it is the "right" reaction.

Another aspect of this characteristic among ACODs is that they have access to a wide range of feelings, not just one or two. Some ACODs complain that they know sadness or fear, but are otherwise numb. Not so the ACOD whose parental divorce experience was positive. They feel a range of emotions. They know frustration, irritation, depression, grief, anger, concern, loving, joy. There are more nuances to their feelings. They do not need an explosive feeling to knock them over the head to know they are alive. Again, these ACODs received two messages from their divorcing parents. One was that it was safe to feel during the divorce process. It was normal to feel. The second was that their own parents had feelings, and they shared them. Feelings were a legitimate part of the divorce process, and not to be controlled out of existence.

ACODs who have access to their feelings believe it is one of the greatest gifts of the divorce process to them, for the divorce was a period of intense feeling and processing of feelings.

Suffering Is Not Romanticized

There is a decided lack of the dramatic among ACODs for whom parental divorce was a positive experience. They watched their parents come to the conclusion that the marriage was not a healthy option, and with that realization, they saw them take firm action. This is not the case in families where parents "stayed together for the sake of the kids." Many of these ACODs can create suffering out of the most trivial relationships. They believe you don't care if you don't suffer.

ACODs from positive parental divorces have had their share of troubles, to be sure. Some went on to intensely troubled relationships, and a fair share of real tragedy. The difference is that they simply do not hang on to suffering, nor do they romanticize it. They take life's events as they come. They are neither blasé nor grandoise about their lives. They tend to live one day at a time. When they tell the story of their parents' divorce, one does not hear that they feel sorry for themselves. They have a ready acceptance of their reality, and they do not deny the parts that were painful.

An ACOD who was brutally beaten by her father when he was in a drunken rage was subsequently raised by loving grandparents who lived in the country. This woman believes that, without the divorce, she would not have fallen into the care of this wonderful couple who nurtured her out of terror and into a healthy life. She tells the story of her abuse in a straightforward manner, and with no self-pity. When you hear her story, you wonder how she survived. She did, and she is clear that without her grandparents, she would be dead. She suffered, and now it is over, and this event from childhood takes its rightful place with other formative events.

Learning to Accept Change

Many ACODs resist change. Their childhood experiences were painful, and pain and change are connected in their minds. Change made it difficult to keep control, and control is a central issue for ACODs. While the divorce itself ended an unpleasant situation, some prefer the familiar dysfunctional family to the unknown healthy one.

Divorce forces change. It alters every aspect of children's existence; which adults will be in their lives, where they will live, where they will spend holidays, what schools they will attend, what friends they'll have, whose faces will be in the family portraits. Divorce, perhaps more than any other event except death, teaches that life is a process.

ACODs who are positive about their experience of their parents' divorce say they were initially wrenched by the changes that the divorce produced. They mourned the loss of their security. At the same time, their worlds broadened, and they began to see that their perspective was not the only perspective. An ACOD whose father divorced to marry another woman remembers how surprised she was by the new wife. "She was so different from my mother that I could not fathom what my father saw in her. I believed that he had to marry someone like Mom, only without her problems. His remarriage forced me to reexamine everything I had believed about my father. I saw that my desire for a woman like Mom was my way of blocking the change in our family. In fact, this new woman was forming an entirely new family with Dad. Things were not going to stay the same, no matter what my little head thought."

Because ACODs face dramatic personal change early in life, some say they are more prepared as adults. Said one ACOD, "My first reaction is always the same. I hate change, I wish I didn't have to go through it. Once I'm past that stage, I look to see what the change is about, and I don't block it. I know I cannot control what is happening around me, and that is a relief."

These ACODs are flexible in the face of differences. They

experienced various styles of living in multiple families. They know their preferences. They have learned that the world is diverse, for their own little universe is teeming with differences. Although initially wary in relationships, they are not shocked to find someone acting other than they expected. "I just try to roll with the punches," mused one ACOD rather philosophically. "You never can predict how things will be. It's just easier to take them as they come."

Whether sought or resisted, change has been a constant in the lives of all ACODs. Those who resisted are troubled today with the fallout from their controlling behavior. Those who accepted change seem to go through life with a noticeable ease, perhaps even a serenity. They have learned to let go. As a consequence, their lives are less restricted and the world is not a fearful place. They walk more effortlessly through life's events. They say they learned how as a result of the divorce.

Experience Different Styles of Child Rearing

"Coming from a divorced family was a virtual laboratory in child rearing," explained a thirty-year-old ACOD who is pregnant with her first child. "One thing divorce will teach you is that there are many ways to deal with children." Interestingly enough, ACODs were both the observers and the subjects of these different styles. (Books on divorce are filled with admonitions to parents to maintain consistency in rules as children go between parents.) Many of the ACODs I interviewed felt that even in the most consistent environments, they still perceived great differences in how their parents cared for them, and overall, they found the experience of these differences was positive for their own development.

Perhaps for the first time, children of divorce saw their parents as individuals, not as a unit. They began to appreciate their separateness. A woman ACOD reflected on what she learned as a child about money. She lived with her father, who believed in searching for ways to give her what she wanted (such as an education at a certain college), even if it was beyond his ability to fund it. He was also generous with gifts. Her mother, on the other hand, believed that her daughter should learn financial responsibility by earning her own tuition. She was willing to contribute something toward college expenses, but not the full amount needed. The young woman did go to the college of her choice, because of the support of her father. Looking back on the two styles, the woman believes she saw the strengths and weaknesses of both. She feels she learned that she could count on her father for financial backup, that he was available to her, and this was a concrete way of showing his caring. She also felt freer to ask her father for things. It was not such a "big deal." From her mother, she learned responsibility, and concern for the cost of things. She learned not to take money for granted. She has combined her learnings in her own life in this way: She is careful about money, and she does not overspend when she is low on money. By the same token, she is generous and feels that she will expect her own children to take financial responsibility, and she intends to help them, especially with big projects like college.

Divorce gives children an experience of different styles in almost every aspect of family life. As they go between families, they form opinions of what works and what does not. Early in life, the opinions are self-centered. Later, children appreciate certain values and carry these forward into their families. Said one ACOD, "My father wanted me to be so good around his new wife. He was always lecturing me in private about my behavior. Then I was supposed to come out and act like a prince. This was not very effective, because I believed that he was ashamed of me. On the other hand, my mother spoke up when I was acting up. She spoke to me in front of my new stepfather. I felt it was okay to be myself in my mother's home. I felt I was not okay in my father's house. I have really learned from my experience. I deal with my own children in the open. I do not want them to grow up thinking I am ashamed of them." Later in life, ACODs appreciate limits, even when they rebelled as youngsters. One man remembers that when he visited his father, he stayed up as late as he wished, whereas his mother had a regular bedtime for him. As a child, he loved the freedom of his father's house. In retrospect, he sees that he did not know his needs for rest and sleep. His mother's rule enabled him to get the sleep he needed, and his days were better with Mom than with Dad.

ACODs benefit from diverse experiences of child rearing. As they raise their own children, they believe they have a wide range of experience to fall back on. Although some of the differences they encountered were painful, even confusing, in adulthood they are able to choose practices they believe worked in the long run. This is one of the surprising benefits of divorce. For those who made it an opportunity and not just a tragedy, they gained invaluable insight into their own experience at the hands of two separate parents, which they then translate into practices that work for them.

Experience Different Lifestyles

Divorce gave ACODs a wide range of options when it came to lifestyles. At the very least, Mom's and Dad's were the first two separate lifestyles after divorce, but in many cases there were more. Many ACODs had parents who divorced more than once. With each new partner came an explosion of new grandparents and relatives. ACODs' flexibility was often tested to the limit in the changing form of the family, and as they participated in ever new arrangements.

Some of the differences in lifestyles were drastic, as in the case of the girl who lived with her mother in abject poverty, and whose father sent a limousine to pick her up for weekly visits.

In other families, there were differences in emphasis. An ACOD whose parents divorced when he was fourteen noticed that his father believed one should work, regardless of job satisfaction, because "without a job, you are nothing." His mother believed one should search for the right job, and that it was worth the time and effort to find suitable work. Prior to the divorce, his father's style had dominated the household. After the divorce, his mother came into a sense of herself, and for the first time the son had an opportunity to see two very different approaches to making a living. He watched his father diminish as he persisted in a job that was not right for him, while his mother flourished in her newfound profession as an interior designer. She had started out slowly, but her business grew as she worked wholeheartedly for its success. She loved her work. "I really don't believe my mother would have taken these risks without the divorce," the son admitted. "And without the divorce, I would never have seen these two different styles that have greatly influenced my choices." Similar to their experiences with different child-rearing practices, ACODs feel they tasted different forms of expression in lifestyle, and this expanded experience provided them with more information from which to choose their own path.

On every indicator of family life, ACODs saw differences. "Try holidays," said one group of ACODs. "I've gone from traditional Thanksgiving with turkey, dressing, and pumpkin pie, to tofu turkey with seeds and nuts pressed into a gluelike substance that was 'good for us,'" volunteered one man whose father remarried a very traditional woman, while his mother joined a health-food commune. "I've gone from dinner tables where children were to be seen and not heard, to tables where you were expected to communicate, to a family where we never sat down to a common meal at all," offered another ACOD.

Is it any wonder that ACODs have great potential both for rigidity and for directionlessness built into the same psyche? Those who emerged battered from the divorce process tend to drift or grab tightly on to anything that will stabilize their unpredictable world. Those who navigated the divorce process with a sense of self intact, however, have a richness of experience that no school could hope to duplicate. They live the process of their lives with a wisdom beyond their years.

Know They Have Choices

"I wasn't glad the divorce happened, but I sure learned lessons I wouldn't have otherwise," said a man whom I interviewed at a conference. "And for what I learned, I am happy, because my folks' split began the process for me." This man learned he had choices at all levels of his life.

First, he learned that he had the choice to remain in a marriage or leave it. Prior to the divorce, he said he felt that marriage commitments were forever, and nothing should break them. Although the divorce rate was growing in society, his true feeling was that divorce was not a choice, it was a failure. It happened to you, you were not in charge. Learning that he was free to leave a commitment resulted in his awareness that he was also free to stay.

Many ACODs relate stories in which one parent grows as a result of divorce, while the other stagnates. These ACODs believe they have the choice to make something from the events of their lives, rather than to pout and mope over the reality they have been dealt. "My parents were a study in contrasts," said an ACOD. "My father turned a new leaf. He became more communicative and open with us kids. He traveled, developed hobbies, and seemed younger and lighter as a person. My mother crawled into a shell and would not come out. She did not maintain her friendships. She let herself go physically. She was massively depressed. I feel like I was watching a drama unfold before me, and I knew I could choose my role. In my life, I could go either way, like my father or mother. Seeing the differences helped me choose my own path in life, as well as an open attitude toward life."

The divorce process sets before ACODs a plethora of choices. They see different styles of relating and communicating. They observe adults reexamining priorities about everything: work, leisure, spirituality, friends. ACODs are quick to point out that they are living their lives differently from their parents in a number of ways, and they learned they had the choice to be different through the divorce process.

Know They Do Not Have to Endure Unhealthy Relationships

With crystal clarity, children of divorce learn this lesson above all else: They can walk away from unhealthy relationships. The ability to leave a dysfunctional relationship is a distinguishing characteristic of the ACOD who experienced divorce positively. Many ACODs have not resolved their relationship issues and perpetuate their family patterns in all their relationships, but some learn this basic lesson through the divorce process: When it is unhealthy, you can leave.

A thirty-nine-year-old woman told me how three generations of her family have used their learning from divorce to become healthier in relationships. Her own family of origin was severely dysfunctional. There was constant violence, and she prayed for her parents' separation so the battering would end, yet the parents did not divorce until the children were grown and gone from home. The one sane feeling she brought from her family was this: "Isn't it more realistic to call this 'divorce' than preserve the romantic fantasy that we are a family?" This realization was the start of the woman's own divorce process. It helped her see that she did not have to suffer most of her life, as her parents did. The woman subsequently divorced her husband, who retained custody of their two children. "My son asked me, 'Why are you leaving us?' I said, 'Your father and I cannot communicate.' And then my son said, 'Whisper in my ear, and I will tell Father.' But I said, 'My son, this business your father and I will do with each other.' My son looked relieved." On Mother's Day, this nine-year-old son wrote to his mother, saying, "Mommy, I'm so glad you can laugh again." The woman says she sees the healing in her family because she had the courage to leave a relationship. She feels she has reversed the earlier dysfunctional family pattern. She believes her children will not commit to others in the way their grandparents did. In fact, last week her son said, "I will handle my own life, Mom, don't do it for me."

Scores of ACODs tell stories in which a battered or abused spouse packs up and leaves, with no obvious means of support. It is as if a light goes on in a youngster's head. "Of course, we don't have to put up with this." Often these situations are not so dramatic. In many instances, a parent acknowledged the relationship was dead. There was nothing there. Accomplishing these separations took courage, because they are harder to explain, yet ACODs are unanimous on this point: Enduring dysfunction does not make you a better person. The denial of your own process, however slight, usually results in unhealthy relationships.

Another aspect of learning in this area is that ACODs sometimes have to look beyond their parents to find caring people. The divorce teaches that neither the mother or father may be able to parent adequately for a time. In the healthy divorce, children received the message that it is all right to receive nurturance from others. Where children risked speaking their needs to grandparents, school counselors, or friends, they often found ready support. Just the acknowledgment that

Mom and Dad could not parent seemed to be a breakthrough for ACODs, who let themselves find support elsewhere.

ACODs extend their learning about relationships to all areas of their lives. Some say they are not as likely to put up with unreasonable demands at work. Lest we believe that ACODs are fleeing every difficult situation they face, it is important to remember that *enduring* is the issue here. Many ACODs distinguish enduring from working things through. They are committed to working toward solutions, but when it is apparent there is no solution, they let go. This is quite different from those who endure and suffer, usually making everyone else suffer, as well.

Learned to Ask for Help

While writing this book, I heard a report on a radio program that cited research indicating that divorce was harmful to children. The researchers had evidence that ACODs sought therapy more frequently than persons from nondivorcing families. The researchers' conclusion was that ACODs were more troubled than non-ACODs. I consider this conclusion ridiculous, and typical of researchers who use data to support their own biases. There are many reasons why ACODs seek therapy. One may be that they are more aware than others that they need help. Also, many divorcing families wisely seek outside help during this time of upheaval. My own opinion is that persons from intact families may be just as troubled as ACODs. The difference is that they do not seek therapy as readily.

ACODs for whom divorce was positive have a realistic estimate of their own strengths and weaknesses. In many cases, facilitators helped families talk through their differences. During divorce, parents encouraged their children to seek therapy, if it would help them. ACODs approach therapy not with a sense that they are crazy but with a sense that they need special support during a time of crisis. This, it seems to me, is a healthy response, not a sign of instability. Even those ACODs who were battered and sexually abused, and who sought support for working through these issues, evidence openness and self-awareness. Many ACODs join Twelve Step recovery programs to deal with drug, alcohol, relationship, and overeating problems, to name a few. In all these cases, the theme is the same. ACODs do not hide out in noble isolation. They admit their needs, and they seek help so as not to repeat the cycle of dysfunction. I believe this willingness to admit the need for help is a strength in ACODs, and it makes a great deal of difference in their ability to lead more productive lives. Those who experienced divorce as a positive solution say they first acknowledged their need for help during the divorce process. Without the divorce, they would neither have sought nor received the assistance that has made a noticeable difference in their lives.

ACODs Show Us the Future

A dualistic perspective does not work when one is studying the effects of divorce on adults, years later. All attempts at simplifying data are confounded by the experience of ACODs. There are some divorces that were so horrendous that we wonder why the offspring went on living. Yet, here they are before me, as lively as those who had every opportunity offered by society and family. Others came from "enlightened" families where the divorce was done "right," yet they are racked with self-doubt and fear of abandonment. Who can predict the outcome with such a mix of variables? Their experience speaks volumes, however. Not all divorce was disastrous. Even the worst had their positive lessons. In the end, I believe divorce can be partially positive and partially negative. ACODs get both good and bad habits and behaviors out of their parents' divorce.

Children of divorce entered adulthood with new eyes about relationships, suffering, choices, and change. They achieved independence and resilience and knew enough to know when they needed help. In our society, we have tended to pity the children of divorce, believing that somehow they missed out on something essential. They were handicapped. But if, indeed, divorce is a process, and a process that is integrally related to a wider societal process, could it be that ACODs are developing exactly the survival skills needed for this new era? It is true that some ACODs are bitterly unhappy about the events of their childhood. The process surely went awry. Still, many others learned valuable lessons. Rather than being handicapped, they feel more astute about life and family. For all we know, they are the forerunners of new family forms. ACODs say they have divorce to thank for their awareness. How ironic if the experience of divorce, an experience most of us would wish to avoid, is one of the processes that best equip us to be healthier in our relationships in the future. For at least a segment of ACODs, this has been the case. Divorce has positive outcomes; those ACODs who could see the possible positive opportunities do not regret it.

The Myth of the Intact Family

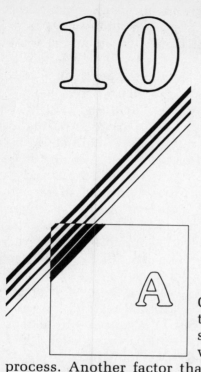

ACODs are not affected just by their families and their family system. Not all of the pain of divorce comes from the divorce process. Another factor that has perpetuated the destructiveness of divorce is that we live in a society that is in denial about the prevalence of divorce, and that touts the ideal of the intact family. Thus, some ACODs feel doubly battered. They were battered by their experience inside the family, and they are also battered by the cultural myth of the intact family.

Many ACODs told me that they felt deficient because they came from divorced families. They carried a social stigma that, I believe, amounts to cultural abuse. Consequently, no exploration of ACOD issues would be complete without a look at the myth of the intact family. ACODs tend to focus their efforts at recovery on themselves and their families of origin. Understanding the role of society in their feelings broadens the picture and facilitates the healing.

ACODs are not the only ones intensely preoccupied with issues of family. Everywhere I went while writing this book, I encountered people in pain about the family, and eager, almost insistent, about talking about their experiences. Almost always I heard in their stories a longing for something other than what they presently have. Why, I wondered, is there such high feeling connected to the topics of family, divorce, and adult children of divorce?

I believe the sensitive nerve I touched was not just a nostalgic longing for the family of old, a television memory. I believe I touched the angst of scores of adults who have labored under an impossible burden, the burden of failing to live up to the myth of the intact family. Their pain could be dismissed as paranoid if it was theirs individually. But it is not. The myth of the intact family is a societal myth and it permeates the society's cultural psyche. Consequently, those who speak with me about their failed relationships and their ACOD struggles often speak as if they have failed not just themselves and their own ideals but something larger, the expectation of the society. Indeed, many ACODs who also divorced attest to these feelings. A forty-year-old woman said, "I know, rationally, that my divorce was in my best interests and for the good of my children. And I had learned from my ACOD experience that I had choices. I did not have to remain in a dysfunctional situation. Yet when I divorced, I felt like I had failed and that I had not lived up to something. It wasn't my own standard I had violated. It was a standard larger than myself. It was a social expectation, and I felt I did not have what it takes."

The myth of the intact family weighs heavily on those who are from the so-called intact families. Many men and women whose parents remained together observed to me that they felt they had the same characteristics as ACODs. As I explored the similarities with them, it became clear that they grew up in homes in which their parents remained married, but the extensive dysfunction of their relationship resulted in their being emotionally divorced. Like the form of divorce where parents stayed together for the sake of the kids, this situation is doubly confusing because the family looks intact on the outside while being "divorced" on the inside. Still, many parents invested in the myth of the intact family, believing that it would carry them through years of dysfunction. Thus, children grew up in families where their parents had dead marriages. Either because of religion or ethnic considerations, they would never have considered divorce. Perhaps they should have. The children of these unions are thoroughly confused about marriage and family. They believe there must be more intimacy in a marriage, but they certainly never saw it. Like ACODs, these children feel they have little knowledge of true intimacy. Having so rarely seen it, they shy away from attempting it for themselves.

Families that stay together but are dysfunctional tend to glorify suffering. Children from these unions tell me they believed that close relationships were supposed to be difficult. They learned that relationships were a source of pain and unhappiness. When they loved someone, it was not supposed to be easy. The measure of their love was their degree of suffering.

Here is the story of Sal, a man whose parents never divorced. I was struck by his story because his first words to me were, "My parents' marriage was over five years after the wedding, and the actual separation took over fifty years and then was only acknowledged with my mother's death." From the outside, his family probably looked good. They were interesting people, the type others admired, but the pain of keeping things intact took quite a toll on family members. Everyone suffered in maintaining the myth.

Sal's mother came from a family of gifted and brilliant women. Her mother was an acclaimed concert pianist, and her sister a well-known journalist. Sal's mother had a passion for art and began painting in her teens. She went to school and majored in biochemistry and planned on a career as a lab technician. Two weeks before graduation she married Sal's father, a physician, and did not graduate.

At five, Sal remembers that he lost all sense of family as a place of shared experience and flexibility. His realization coincided with Sal's father's beginning an affair with his secretary, an affair that was to last for years. At this time, Sal became overwhelmed with a sense of disillusionment. He hid at school and he dreaded going home. He felt confused about his parents.

By the time Sal reached eighteen years of age, his father was drinking heavily and becoming more isolated with his affair. His medical practice was floundering. Sal's mother began painting again and her work was dark—predominantly women with no faces and no arms. They were dull and lacked personality. The family was focused on the father's drinking. His disease pervaded their lives and affected almost everything they did. About this time, Sal's mother asked Sal if he thought she should divorce his father. Sal felt important and terrified to be taken into his mother's confidence in this way. He said, "Yes, I think you should divorce Dad." To this day, he feels important and terrified when someone asks him for advice. But Sal's mother chose not to divorce, and Sal remembers that all the photographs from the time she decided against divorce are of a woman whose face is set, lined, and careworn.

Sal's mother disappeared further into her art, his father into his drinking, smoking, and his affair. Sal and his two brothers felt increasingly abandoned. Their father was undependable and their mother was unavailable. She immersed herself in classes and trips to the museum. She found an institutionalized sanctuary in the art world, a place to escape. Slowly, her vitality returned, and near the end of her life she painted exciting and colorful pieces, most of them landscapes.

Sal's mother died of lung cancer due to the secondary smoke from her husband's nicotine addiction. Sal believes she died of caretaking his father. He feels that in some way she did get divorced, for her artwork was a way of separating. Yet there is great sadness about Sal. He says that if he could have witnessed his mother making a clear, life-giving choice, it would have been a model for him. Her decision not to divorce was not really a decision because afterward she did nothing to change the situation. She merely escaped into her art, leaving her children and her responsibility for her part in the relationship with Sal's father. She did not make a choice that enhanced her own spirit. As a result, Sal feels he has much unfinished business in his own life. He longs for a model of adults who take responsibility for themselves and their choices, who move through a process and even when painful, learn and are more alive afterward. He mourns the years his mother wasted her vigor and her artistic gift.

Sal says that his mother, by not divorcing, actually separated from a part of her own spirituality. She made the choice to stay with her husband, then divorced her own spirit to do it. In the process, she lost herself. Her children feel they lost her energy and attention as a parent. They were an intact family that, in truth, was divorced from their liveliness and their feelings, from one another and ultimately from themselves. The form of staying together was not enough to support them emotionally.

As Sal thinks about divorce, he says he feels that the way we use the word "divorce" is inaccurate. He thinks the term connotes a severing, that one is getting rid of something, that it is final. This, he suggests, is rarely the case as the relationships, and the effects of relationships, continue on for years. Perhaps Sal is right; divorce no longer stands solely for the severing of a marriage relationship. Like cancer, divorce has become a metaphor for deeper processes in ourselves, our relationships, and society. The refusal to admit that the intact family is not a panacea for society's ills, and that, in fact, it is less and less common, prevents us from recognizing and exploring other alternatives to the intact family.

How does society perpetuate the myth of the intact family? In large part, it does so through a series of assumptions that, I believe, have until now gone largely unexamined.

The first societal assumption states that staying together in long-term relationships is good; short-term relationships are bad. This assumption underlies a double standard that is actively supported by the major religious groups and the civil society itself. It is reflected in vows in which couples promise "till death do us part." The standard is the commitment to the long-term relationship. The reality is that fewer and fewer people remain in such relationships. The major social and religious institutions choose to look the other way rather than face the reality that long-term relationships may no longer be as viable as they once were.

Because of the spread of AIDS, we are told that there is a rise in monogamy and a second baby boom. Yet even with a return to traditional values, the divorce rate remains constant at one out of two marriages. We keep trying the nuclear family, but we are not becoming more successful at it.

All around us we see a world that is changing, and it is changing with a rapidity unknown to previous generations.

Our beliefs about longevity seem to lag behind our experience. In the United States, many people will change occupations seven times in their lifetime, and a majority of the population changes residence or geographic location every five years. In a research study I did of urban communes in Boston in the early 1970s, I found that 80 percent of the urban commune dwellers considered two years a "long time" to have the same group in a house. Their usual experience was a turnover of housemates every six months.

The belief that long-term relationships are good, short-term bad, sets longevity as an external standard against which to measure ourselves. Neither long-term nor short-term is good nor bad. When, as a society, we value one over the other, we are not open to possibilities for other forms for relationships. We persist in our determination that the family of old is possible. Moreover, we establish the traditional family as the ideal and measure every other relational form against it. This assumption prevents us from looking at our reality and working within it.

Inevitably, if we abandoned our assumptions about relationships, there would continue to be those who entered into long-term relationships and stayed in them over the years. Others would move in and out as they needed. In a society that valued the process of relating rather than a static standard of the "right" relationship, all forms of relating would receive appropriate support. In addition, the guilt and shame that many ACODs now carry because they cannot meet the societal expectation would be greatly reduced.

A woman who was the first person in five generations of her family to divorce said that she remained in an intolerable marriage for years because "in my family we just don't get divorced, no matter what. It is not an option." After her divorce, she was subtly ostracized from her family. She said, "I felt relief at being out of the situation with my former husband, and I was proud that I could take care of myself. But with my family it was as if I had taken my finger from the dike. My divorce made possible the same action for other family members who were equally miserable. For this, I experienced a lot of guilt and felt blamed for years."

A second societal assumption states that a society in

which people will live to age seventy-five can operate with the same relationship commitments as a society in which people live to age forty-five. Surely, the kinds of marriages and the relationship expectations a culture has for those who will spend only twenty years together are different for those who can conceivably live almost twice as long. Our societal expectations for marriage seem to be based on life in the 1850s, rather than the 1990s.

Like present societies, earlier societies experienced war, chaos, and political upheavals. Yet, in those earlier periods, the family, extended families, and communities appeared to be a bulwark against the outside world. We like to believe the family was a place of safety, into which one could retreat from the hazards of society. However, historical studies of the family are raising questions about just how ideal the family of old really was. There is evidence that women and children did not fare well and that physical abuse was as common in the pre-twentieth-century family as it is today.

Perhaps all we can conclude is that prior to the late 1950s, there was tremendous societal and community pressure on husbands and wives to stay together. Judith Wallerstein, quoting a conversation with Margaret Mead, says that our society is radically different because "we have created in the last twenty years *a world in which marriage is freely terminable at any time for the first time in history."* [1] Moreover, with the relative loss of societal pressure to stay together, the nature of our stress differs from our predecessors'. They seemed to bond in the face of cultural upheaval; we seem to fragment. Rather than becoming a haven, the intact family is a victim of cultural distress.

We expect to adjust to change in every sphere of science, technology, and the environment. The most dramatic change is in the complexity of the human psyche. How can we expect that the choices we make at twenty-one are still appropriate at fifty or at eighty, not to mention all the decades in between?

Everything around us has changed since the turn of the century, yet the culturally bound expectation of long-term relationships seems blind to the fact that the human person is not the same in needs, expectations, and skills. A great deal of the emotional investment in the myth of the intact family comes from a rigid adherence to modes of thought based on an earlier time and a shorter life span. This adherence keeps us in denial about our experience, which does not coincide with earlier cultural experience, nor with the myths about marriage and divorce that we inherited from that time.

The third societal assumption is that the family is the basic social unit and it should be strengthened. Underlying this assumption is the understanding that "family" usually refers to a mother, father, and children.

I believe we must question the assumption that the family is the basic social unit. As the earlier section of this book demonstrates, most ACODs have years of unfinished personal work related to their experience of living in a dysfunctional family. There is no question that the way many are experiencing family today is detrimental to the family members. Should the family as a primary social unit be strengthened? And if it were, would it make a difference?

I think we need to examine such issues as the isolation of the family, our mobile society, and the corporate world. All of these militate against the integrity of the traditional family unit. Families are without the support of older generations and relatives. Mobility keeps people from establishing roots in neighborhoods and from developing the support groups that could enhance family life. The corporate world of business is driven by a basic concern for profit, which results in workaholic standards for those who choose a career there. The family is a casualty of those trends. Although political leaders claim to be profamily, little real support in the form of legislation has been enacted that would actually have strengthened this floundering family unit. Again, the rhetoric of "family" is for the purpose of supporting the myth of the intact family. Yet what is going on in these intact families?

Everywhere I go I hear that the family is in trouble. Educators complain they are now performing tasks of physical care and emotional nurturing that rightfully belong to parents, but are not being done at home. Violence is reported in 38 percent of families, and there is increasing awareness of incest. Multiple addictions are found in almost every family. In just twenty years, we have witnessed "broken families," single-parent families, and lately parentless families as crack-cocaine-addicted parents have neither the inclination nor the ability to parent their offspring.

I believe our adherence to the myth of the intact family prevents us from acknowledging the existence and the viability of the many alternatives as legitimate family forms. If the society were to respond to the fact that a great variety of family forms exist—single parents by divorce, single parents by choice, unmarried couples with children, gay and lesbian parents, grandparents, aunts and uncles raising children— perhaps there would be some help for the family. However, little is done to develop or foster other social units. This is unfortunate because to admit the reality of such forms would benefit parents, children, and ultimately the society itself.

We can hardly ignore the fact that "Mom, Pop, and the kids" is rapidly becoming a minority family form, while other arrangements are on the rise. I believe that the traditional family has been declining as the basic social unit for at least twenty years.

A fourth societal assumption is that divorce results in disturbed children and dysfunctional adults. This is an assumption that needs to be challenged, both from the popular view and the research perspective.

My experience in interviewing persons from both divorced and intact families is that dysfunction is present in both situations. We cannot ignore that there are massive numbers of ACODs who do well in all aspects of their lives. Also, we need to ask, How many people had problems before they married? In many cases, divorce is not the main issue. It is not even the cause of dysfunction. Divorce was the result of previously existing dysfunction.The issue for many adult children of divorce is not just that their parents divorced. It is the effect that the dysfunctional parent had on the child.

We need to question the level of denial in the society when we believe that divorce results in dysfunctional adults and children, while giving less weight to the numbers of intact families where affairs are common, marriages feel dead, and abuse is an everyday occurrence. We also need to question our persistence in believing that the intact family is the norm and divorce is the problematic exception. Twenty years of statistics on divorce now show that divorce *is* very common. It is the choice of 50 percent of all people who marry. The function of denying the prevalence of divorce is to prevent us from taking steps to claim divorce as a very real aspect of relational life among people. It is a normal response and a viable choice. To deny this keeps the society focused on one marriage form and one type of family unit that may not be the best solution. It is to prop up one option of relating, while ignoring the possibilities inherent in the other, divorce. We abhor divorce at the cost of maintaining our myth about the supremacy of the intact family. Regrettably, the dysfunction of intact families is not clearly seen, so troubled families do not receive help, just as children and adults of divorce do not get the support they need to move on to healthier situations.

Our language gives us away. We speak of children of divorce as coming from "broken families." We keep the intact family myth alive with such language. It has been interesting to me to be around people who describe themselves as coming from intact dysfunctional families. This seems an honest description, yet it does not carry the social stigma that "broken" does. Broken implies a need to be fixed. This language ignores that divorce may have been positive.

Finally, we have to question the manner in which research in the area of divorce reflects the bias of the society in favor of the intact family. Several research studies on children of divorce claim that ACODs become divorced themselves, and that they seek therapy and see themselves as damaged by divorce. The assertion that ACODs become divorced themselves is an interesting interpretation because 50 percent of all people who marry eventually divorce. These are massive numbers, and it is not surprising that ACODs would be among them. Indeed, for many ACODs, divorce may be the healthy alternative, and not a failure. Unfortunately the research carries the implication that children of divorce are flawed and therefore make a flawed choice themselves.

Another set of data claims that children of divorce see themselves as more damaged and subsequently seek help more frequently than persons from intact families. Earlier, I discussed my belief that we have to allow for the fact that ACODs are not more dysfunctional than persons from intact families. The reality may be that they are more open to receiving help and seek it out, whereas children of intact families are more isolated in their families and more into denial. The other factor that research does not seem to account for in self-reporting studies of children of divorce is their reaction to social stigma. Many ACODs reported feeling different and ashamed of being from a divorced family. Whenever religion figured prominently in an ACOD's childhood, the stigma was even greater. (This indicates, perhaps, that churches are the last place we should look to for leadership in dealing with issues of divorce.) Thus, children of divorce may see themselves as more damaged because society sees them as damaged. Whether they really are more damaged or not is not clear. The point here is that researchers report these results as if they were true. I believe there is no basis for drawing the conclusion that children of divorce are categorically more damaged than children from intact families, and I think that such judgments only reflect the bias of the researcher.

Overall, research in this area has tended to get caught in dualistic thinking by comparing children from "broken homes" to those from intact homes. There are at least four forms within the basic two of "divorce" and "intact." There are functional and dysfunctional intact families, and functional and dysfunctional divorced families.

I believe that comparing children of divorce to children of intact families oversimplifies a complex reality. It makes family a static thing rather than a process. When stasis is valued, change is always experienced as wrenching and thus to be feared. But when family is seen as a process, not just a thing, then divorce may be a healthy response to the preservation of such qualities as mutual respect and love. It may be the best way to support the preciousness of the life of the family members.

When family is a process and not a thing, "divorced" and "intact" become irrelevant. The issue is being fully alive in oneself, and taking responsibility for oneself and the relationships one chooses. Staying together or separating is an outcome of that choice, but neither divorce nor remaining married is the end. They are only the means to wholeness of selves and families.

Research in the area of children of divorce should be

approached gingerly. Much of it still reflects a bias for the intact family and consequently, interprets findings about children of divorce against that standard. Rarely are studies conducted on the problems of the intact family that consider the effects on children of living in families where marriages are dead or where parents stay together for the sake of the children. Until such studies are made, our picture of the effects on children of a realistic range of family dynamics is very incomplete.

In the early stages of my interviewing ACODs, I was focused primarily on their feelings and the behaviors they developed in response to divorce in their families. Their stories were absorbing, gripping, humorous, and painful. Over time, I began to hear a common theme from many ACODs. For some it was a sense of shame that they came from divorced families; for others it was a longing to belong to a normal family. For almost all of them, it was the belief that the intact family was something to be sought and hopefully achieved sometime in life. The force of this expectation led me to examine the role of the society in perpetuating such intense desire.

I began to see the enormous investment our society has in maintaining the myth of the intact family, and I must confess that I am persuaded that the intact family is greatly idealized. I do not dispute that millions of people are married. I question how functional that form is. I question its viability in our rapidly changing culture, and I wonder at the intensity with which so many hold on to it. I am astounded at the longing I find in many ACODs to achieve a "normal" family when such an entity rarely exists.

Unfortunately, all of the societal assumptions propping up the myth of the intact family result in most social institutions' denying the inevitability and normalcy of divorce. Consequently, our social institutions do not provide either the support or the network to make a divorce experience constructive. As long as there persists such denial in the society, those who could benefit from help go unaided.

I believe that as our attempts to live out the myth of the intact family fail, the social system evolves solutions to our deepest problems. For so long, we have believed divorce was a problem, a shame, and a dysfunction. Perhaps it is a healthy response to an outmoded social structure. The concomitant development of multiple family forms, which are growing everywhere, promises alternatives to the traditional family. Some have observed that the nuclear family cannot survive without something around it. The nuclear family exists in a vacuum. It needs to be held in place by a support structure outside itself. The myth of the intact family has precipitated this distress for the nuclear family by isolating it into a form unto itself.

Regardless of what family forms ACODs and others choose, all people need support for their relationships and for taking responsibility for their own lives. The intact family will become a reality when it takes its place on an equal footing with other family forms. Hopefully, we will drop such confusing terms as "intact" and "broken," and we will be "family," whatever that means in our individual situations. As the world shrinks, we will extend our notion of family to include the global community. This awareness itself may move us to redefine the size and function of the family unit. It seems to me that throughout society we witness the demise of our illusions about family. This is a process. Although it is painful, it is necessary. We make the process more painful when we resist it. The first step in supporting family in all its forms is to let go of the myth of the intact family. It is essential to do this for the sake of ourselves, our families, and our society.

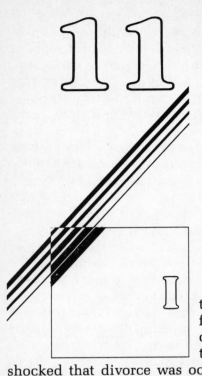

New Attitudes, New Families

It has been twenty years since the first alarming statistics concerning the rate of divorce came to light. In the early seventies, shocked that divorce was occurring in one out of every two marriages, the popular press speculated on a turnaround and a decrease in the divorce rate. From the perspective of twenty years elapsed, it is clear that the early seventies marked the beginning of a trend that is now well entrenched. The divorce rate, at this time, shows no sign of a decrease.

As I review the statistics and let my mind wander over the scores of interviews with ACODs conducted in the preparation for this book, two ACOD qualities impress me: their relief and their resilience. Their relief was evident whenever I named a characteristic. It was as if they had walked out of a dark room into one filled with light and friends. A forty-year-old man writes, "You will never know my gratitude for the opportunity to talk about my experience. The chance to describe my life in my divorcing family represents the cracking of my denial about the effects on me. To realize that other people share some of the same characteristics supports my efforts to heal in so many ways."

186

This man is typical of so many who feel a release just by the process of naming and recognizing the ACOD characteristics. I feel that the powerful response to this naming process tells us that adult children of divorce have been in greater pain than we had understood. In the process of writing this book, I touched a vast sea of unresolved pain on the part of ACODs. At times, even my research assistant and typist complained that the work of this book was "hard." All of us were relieved finally to get to the section on the good news about divorce! Reviewing the ACOD experience, one is tempted to deem the situation hopeless and conclude simply, "What a mess!" My work with ACODs, however, gives me reason to hope.

In the most discouraging ACOD stories there is a surprising resilience. There is a willingness to accept the truth of their family's history. There is an openness to understand how divorce affects them as adults, and there is a discernible resolve to make the life changes necessary to achieve recovery. Because ACODs are aware that they inherited some of their parents' unresolved processes, they seem to have a special concern for future generations. It is in this that they bear a striking similarity to one another. They say without fail, "I want to understand myself and heal so my kids aren't hurt as I was." One of the most touching examples of resilience came from a woman in her late sixties. She said, "I know I don't have many more years to live, but the ones I have left I want to be fully alive. I'm going to really work on my ACOD recovery. I want these to be the best years."

Although my purpose in writing this book was to help ACODs by describing their common experience, I found that ACODs taught me much in return. I share some of their lessons because ACODs and non-ACODs alike can profit from the ACOD experience.

In the first place, ACODs confirm what some researchers have been saying for several years, that divorce is long lasting in its effects. Divorce remains a key process for ACODs and is an issue they carry with them throughout their lives.

ACODs teach us that we are indeed a community, and a family. We are not alone, and each of us is irrevocably affected by those closest to us. ACODs were greatly affected by the example of their parents. The parental response to divorce has a profound impact on their children. That parents resorted to fighting, shouting, violence, and the threat of violence is not forgotten by children. Many ACODs admit that their own problems with their aggressiveness stem from blindly acting in the same manner as their divorcing parents. Even those who do not wish to emulate their parents in any way acknowledge that they feel their parents' example is imprinted on their brains.

ACODs show us that the quality of the relationship between their parents played a large part in their own ability to adjust to divorce. In the divorce itself and in its aftermath, ACODs felt safe in situations where parents took responsibility for themselves, and where there were clear boundaries between parent issues and child issues. Where these issues became mixed, children felt the overwhelming burden of caretaking one or both parents.

ACODs are a prime example of the fact that divorce can be a healthy choice. They show us that independence, self-sufficiency, and awareness of choice of lifestyle attends the healthy divorce. As children, ACODs developed competencies that set them apart from their peers who came from intact families.

The primacy of relationships is core to the ACOD experience. A recurring theme of this book is that whenever a person does not take responsibility for him/herself (and that means responsibility for feelings, actions, family history, agreements, and plans), the person suffers, and so do those around him or her. Too many ACODs felt battered in families where the adults did not attend to their own needs and subsequently took out their frustrations on their children. A young man put it this way: "If I've learned one thing from my ACOD background, it is when I don't take care of myself and take responsibility for myself, I am a hazard to myself and others."

This a key lesson in ACOD stories and for their recovery. It would be too easy to find someone to blame, and the culprits are many. ACODs can blame their parents. They didn't do it right. ACODs can blame their grandparents. They can blame the institutions of society. Ultimately, ACODs can blame themselves for being born into such a situation.

ACODs teach us differently. We learn from recovering ACODs that satisfying relationships begin when each family member has a relationship first to the self and then to the other members. Without the relationship to the self as primary, there is no hope for relationship with the other family members. If anything, family is the place where we are presented with the opportunity to form these essential bonds. My experience with ACODs leads me to question whether, indeed, real family exists unless there is this basic, relational life. I have learned from ACODs that whether the family is called intact or divorced, the relational issue is the same. It is the ground of all other issues in the family.

What of the society at large? What can various segments of our society learn from the ACOD experience? Those of us who research and study the family have years of work ahead. Many studies are drawing conclusions about the damaging effects of divorce on children. We need more work on ACODs as well as studies on the effects of the dysfunctional intact family on children. In fact, we do not even have a set of characteristics to describe life in these various family forms. We are recognizing alternative family forms but we have little data on their viability. We need frames of reference and measures that are not derived from the intact family. There is no denying that the intact family is the prevailing model, yet if other forms are compared to it, we continue the expectation that all new forms must be referenced to the traditional family. Then we lose the opportunity to assess alternative families on their own merits.

I believe it is difficult to do research on the family without stimulating deeply held feelings on the part of the researchers. I do not believe there is such a thing as objectivity in relation to this subject; however, I do believe that researchers can be neutral while recognizing their own issues around family. The ACOD issue, which is surely shared by 50 percent of those doing research, must be confronted personally before researchers can approach this topic. Otherwise, the findings tend to reflect and to continue the researchers' biases.

Allan Bloom, in The Closing of the American Mind, decries the decomposition of the bonds between family members as the most urgent social problem in America today. Yet, he observes, he never finds marriage and divorce on any policymaker's agenda.[1]

Social policy has not kept up with social reality. We are still in denial about the numbers of persons no longer in the intact family. Our legislation, tax structure, and welfare system continue the myth, while all around us the numbers of needy increase.

Our social policy is not based on the facts. We have few support systems to help parents and children make the transition from the intact to the divorced family. College-age children from divorced families are still penalized when they apply for financial aid. Fathers' incomes are counted, even though the majority of eighteen-year-olds receive little support from fathers. An enlightened social policy would recognize this fact and do something about it.

Public schools finally began classes in marriage and the family in order to prepare youngsters for the responsibility of adults. Now we need to see classes that prepare youngsters for the range of lifestyle options they will encounter in this decade. ACODs felt most stigmatized at school and in church. Both of these institutions could facilitate healthy adjustment to lifestyle change through discussion and acceptance of the inevitability of divorce. Above all, the churches should cease their judgment against divorce and the family members going through divorce. Too many ACODs said the church was willing to minister to their families as if they were defective. If churches and schools were to comprehend the significance of the ACOD issue, they would serve all people without categorizing them.

Family therapy, to be relevant, needs to come out of the clinic/office and into the home. Too many ACODs report that they could have benefited from the assistance of social workers and counselors but did not know how to find them. ACODs attest to the isolation of the American family. It is alarming to note that as therapy and social welfare systems become more sophisticated, the number of those not receiving the help they need grows. Our helping professions seem unable to respond to changing needs. When the systems cannot adjust, people fall through the cracks.

A fascinating implication of the ACOD issue is that as the usual providers of human services grind into virtual inertia, self-help groups are flourishing. An obvious outcome of ACOD awareness is the appearance of a new array of self-help groups. Already, I know from my ACOD interviews, the ACODs who began recovery most quickly were those who shared their experience with other ACODs in a safe environment. This is an important development and has implications for both "helping" and "family" in the future.

In the absence of social policy and institutional response to ACOD issues, people seek ways to help themselves. As they do, they enter into a community of support, sanity, and examples of healthy relating. For some it is the first time they have been in an environment where they can be themselves and see others act responsibly, where caring is expressed in honest feedback, and where acceptance is authentic, not based on pleasing others. There is no denying that new family forms are all around us, and self-help groups may be the essential support system for them.

Finally, what are the implications of ACOD issues and recovery for our concepts of family? I believe the implications are paradoxical. ACODs teach us that family is no longer one form. Family is relatedness, usually over time. It is a quality of acceptance of others born out of responsibility for the self. ACODs show us that family is found in the most unlikely of places. Although we have believed family was the inevitable result of bonding of two people in marriage, ACODs lead us to question whether this physical, legal bond is the only family.

Surely we are at a critical juncture not only for the ACODs of this study but for the whole human family. Our struggles are to find satisfying, nurturing, and lasting bonds in families. Yet we are not alone. The nature of the problem is holographic. Few of the old theories of history, family dynamics, religion, and gender can hold together, much less explain, the shift we are in. The problems of the globe require concerted response in every locality. The nature of the trauma in families is so large that it demands a societal response. ACODs are just one powerful reminder that family as we have known it is undergoing dramatic change.

The ACOD experience helps us to turn our gaze to a world of other options—beyond our national borders to other nations and cultures where family is the collectivity, the extended group, and those we hold in our hearts, who are not necessarily blood relations.

During a trip to Australia, I spent time with aboriginal

men and women who described their understanding of family. They told me that in the aboriginal tribe/family, each person occupies a unique place. You could leave the family for thirty years and your place would still be there when you returned. In aboriginal society, you can choose to absent yourself from family, but family will not absent itself from you.

I was profoundly touched by this information. I immediately thought about all the ACODs I interviewed. Abandonment was such a major theme for most of them. Abandonment was the sense that no one knew they existed, that if they left the family either physically or psychologically, their "place" in the family closed, disappeared. All too often, becoming healthy in the family was punished by abandonment on the part of the other dysfunctional family members.

Nevertheless, as I contrast the aboriginals to the ACODs of this study, I am still hopeful. We have so much to learn from one another. ACODs have certainly been teachers for me. As they heal, they are a reminder of the resilience of the individual. It is true that ACODs' major concerns are focused on their individual recovery from their divorcing families. Yet I believe that as ACODs heal, they gain the strength to look beyond themselves.

ACODs' focus broadens to include the collectivity and the community. There is room for us all in such a process. ACODs teach us that through naming our reality, feeling our pain, and taking responsibility for ourselves, we also help society.

I believe the process that ACODs go through is also a new paradigm for family and society. I trust their process because I have seen them heal, and because of their example, I know we will come home to ourselves and have, at last, a true family.

NOTES

CHAPTER 1
Adult Children of Divorce—The Problems, the Challenge

1. Larry Bumpass. "Children and Marital Disruption: A Replication and Update." *Demography*, 1984, Vol 21, p. 71–82.
2. Judith S. Wallerstein and Sandra Blakeslee. *Second Chances*. New York: Ticknor and Fields, 1989.

CHAPTER 3
Addiction and the ACOD

1. Sharon Wegscheider-Cruse. *Another Chance: Hope and Health for the Alcoholic Family*. Palo Alto, California: Science and Behavior Books, 1980.
2. Anne Wilson Schaef. *Escape From Intimacy*. San Francisco: Harper and Row, 1989.

CHAPTER 4
Abuse and the ACOD

1. The American Association for Protecting Children. *Highlights of Official Child Neglect*. 1986.
2. Richard J. Gelles and Murray A. Straus. *Intimate Violence*. New York: Simon and Schuster, 1988, p. 91.

CHAPTER 5
Types of Divorce

1. _____. "Never a Right Age." *Scientific American*, September 1987, Vol. 257, p. 32.
2. Wallerstein and Blakeslee, op. cit., p. 176.
3. Gelles and Straus, op. cit., p. 41.

CHAPTER 6
Adult Children of Divorce—The Characteristics

1. Lenore J. Weitzman. *The Divorce Revolution: The Unexpected Social and Economic Consequences for Women and Children in America*. New York: Free Press, 1985.

2. Norval D. Glenn and Kathryn B. Kramer. "The Marriages and Divorces of Children of Divorce." *Journal of Marriage and the Family*, November, 1987, p. 811–25.

3. Verna M. Keith and Barbara Finlay. "The Impact of Parental Divorce on Children's Educational Attainment, Marital Timing, and Likelihood of Divorce." *Journal of Marriage and the Family*, August 1988, p. 797.

4. R. Kulka and H. Weingarten. "Implications of Parental Divorce in Childhood on Adult Adjustment." *Journal of Social Issues*, 1979, Vol 35, p. 50–78.

CHAPTER 10

The Myth of the Intact Family

1. Wallerstein and Blakeslee, op. cit., p. 297.

CHAPTER 11

New Attitudes, New Families

1. Allan Bloom. *The Closing of the American Mind.* New York: Simon and Schuster, 1987.